LAW ENFORCEMENT CAREER STARTER

by Mary N. Hesalroad

LearningExpress ♦ New York

Library of Congress Cataloging-in-Publication Data

Law enforcement career starter: finding and getting a great job.
    p.   cm.
  ISBN 1–57685–111–7
    1. Law enforcement—Vocational guidance—United States.
2. Police—Vocational guidance—United States. I. LearningExpress
(Organization) II. Series.
HV8143.L37   1998
363.2'023'73—dc21   98–3561
                          CIP

Printed in the United States of America
9 8 7 6 5 4 3 2 1
First Edition

Regarding the Information in this Book
Every effort has been made to ensure accuracy of directory information up until press time.
However, phone numbers and/or addresses are subject to change. Please contact the respective organization for the most recent information.

For Further Information
For information on LearningExpress, other LearningExpress products, or bulk sales, please
call or write to us at:
    LearningExpress™
    900 Broadway
    Suite 604
    New York, NY 10003
    212-995-2566

LearningExpress is an affiliated company of Random House, Inc.

ISBN 1-57685-111-7

7 85555 85111 5

CONTENTS

ABOUT THE AUTHOR

Mary N. Hesalroad, a former police officer with over eight years of experience, is a writer and law enforcement consultant living in Austin, Texas. During her policing career she was assigned to the patrol division, motorcycle division, and recruiting/background investigations section.

INTRODUCTION

WHY ENTER THE LAW ENFORCEMENT FIELD?

Law enforcement is one of the hottest career fields around, especially if you are looking for work as a police officer, corrections officer, or special agent. In fact, the U.S. Department of Labor estimates that opportunities in some of these law enforcement career fields will grow faster than the average for all other occupations in the U.S. through the year 2005. Not a bad forecast if you are just starting your career search or considering a move into law enforcement!

Entry-level positions in law enforcement are plentiful, but the competition for these jobs is tough. This book will not only give you the details about the fastest growing fields, it will also show you how to become "the competition" everyone else fears.

Chapter one gives you an idea of the typical salaries earned by local, state, and federal law enforcement professionals. You'll see what the beginning police officers in the fastest growing cities in America are earning, and you'll find out the salaries of federal agents and deputy sheriffs. The often-mysterious application process for law enforcement positions will be explained, and tips for making it through the process will be provided. Chapter one contains detailed information about the jobs, training, and basic requirements for police officers, deputy sheriffs, and corrections officers. We've also included phone numbers and addresses for potential employers in the field. Plus, if you've ever wondered whether you are "the type" to carry a badge and a gun, you'll have an opportunity to take a quick suitability exam at the end of the chapter to help you answer that question. After the test, you'll get an insider's story on what it's like to be a police officer.

Chapter two will let you in on the details of federal employment, including information about the agencies who hire the largest numbers of federal officers, the salaries you can expect, the hiring processes, and points of contact. You'll get descriptions of numerous federal jobs, including information on the necessary qualifications and training. At the end of this chapter, you'll hear advice from a federal agent on how to prepare yourself for a law enforcement career.

One thing all employers of law enforcement have in common is their growing demand for college-educated applicants. Chapter three explores the reasons behind the demand, why an education will pay off in the end, and how to choose the right program of study. It also gives advice from professionals in the education and law enforcement community. To make your decision easier, we've included a list of colleges and universities that offer criminal justice-related programs, with notations marking the schools with ROTC scholarships. At the end of chapter three you'll hear advice from an admissions expert from one of the top criminal justice colleges in the country.

Since higher education is not free in this country, chapter four gives explanations of financial aid, lists of contacts for financial aid programs, and scholarship information. We've also provided a state-by-state listing of higher education and student financial assistance organizations.

Unlike many professions, law enforcement managers are very concerned about the maturity level and life experience that their applicants bring with them into the job. Because of this, fewer and fewer law enforcement agencies are hiring applicants under the age of 21. Does this spell catastrophe for you, or is it a prime opportunity for you to prepare yourself for the challenges ahead? Chapter five takes a look at one option that might give you a chance to do it all: military service. Enlisting in the armed forces enables you to finance your education, improve your maturity, and get life experience. You'll get detailed information on the advantage veterans have in law enforcement hiring, the experience you'll have if you choose the enlisted route, and the strategies for combining higher education and military duty all in one. At the end of this chapter you'll hear from a law enforcement professional in the U.S. Air Force.

Of course, no book on law enforcement careers would be worth its salt without a strategy for how to be a successful law enforcement candidate. Chapter six passes on advice collected from interviews with recruiters and law enforcement managers across the country on what you should do to prepare for the hiring process. You'll get detailed information about how to prepare for the two most intimidating experiences in the application process: the written personal history statement and the oral interview board. Chapter Six ends with comments from one of Audrain County Sheriff's Department's finest.

To help with your career search, your quest for knowledge about educational opportunities, and your military options, Appendix A tells you how to use the World Wide Web to find what you need. You'll get advice from an experienced research librarian and see addresses for the best law enforcement-related sites on the Web. There's even a tip or two on how to conduct your searches. Appendix B contains a listing of FBI field offices. And finally, in Appendix C, we've included a list of publications to further assist you in your job search.

Well, if you haven't already, start flipping these pages! Your search for the law enforcement career of your dreams starts now.

CHAPTER | 1

This chapter examines average salaries, lifestyles, and job opportunities in law enforcement. You'll also learn about the general personality traits and characteristics your future employers look for in new recruits. Basic duties for local and state law enforcement personnel are explored, along with details on minimum requirements, testing procedures, and contact information. You'll even have an opportunity to take a quick test to see if you are suited for this challenging career.

LAW ENFORCEMENT JOBS

What cops and FBI agents do on television looks easy. They work on one case at a time until it's solved and they always get the bad guy—all without putting pen to paper and all in an hour's time. Unless you are lucky enough to get hired on the TV series "The X-Files," you'll just have to settle for real-life law enforcement, complete with reams of paperwork, long hours, and the occasional rush of heart-pounding excitement. The hard part isn't figuring out that law enforcement is a great career, it's figuring out whether this field is for you and, if so, which job is best.

That's why you are here! But before you read much further, you should spend a few minutes taking the Police Officer Suitability Test at the end of this chapter. Although you may be looking for a career with the county, state, or federal government instead of with a municipal police force, this short quiz is great for giving you a ball-park idea of how well you're suited to carry a badge. Even if you chose an office job far from the thrills of street-level policing, you'll still need the skills and characteristics common to all law enforcement professionals. After you take the test, come back and we'll talk money.

TYPICAL SALARIES

Loving what you do for a living is important, and so is being able to make a living at what you love. Law enforcement won't be attractive to you for long if you can't afford to take the job. What you'll earn as a deputy sheriff, police officer, federal agent, or state trooper will vary according to your employer's pocketbook.

The most recent pay information compiled by the U.S. Department of Labor Bureau of Labor Statistics is from 1996. Hold your budget up beside these figures. According to this source, deputy sheriffs around the country made, on the average, around $2,155/month, ($25,862/year); fish and game wardens made close to $2,329/month ($27,955/year); railroad, transit police, and special agents made $2,784/month ($33,408/year) and private security guards made $1,280/month ($15,360/year)—just to look at a few occupations. Keep in mind that these are average salaries reported by agencies and companies nationwide that responded to the Bureau's annual survey.

Since police departments hire more officers than any of the other law enforcement agencies, they deserve a closer look. The number crunchers at the U.S. Bureau of Labor tell us that the chances of getting a job in law enforcement are great through the year 2005. Common sense tells us that the best places to look for these jobs are with local and state agencies that serve areas with increasing populations. With that in mind, we've taken a look at eight agencies among the top ten fastest growing cities in America to give you an idea of what you'd be making if you opted for a career in policing. These are entry-level *base* pay scales and do not include additional money for shift differentials, hazardous duty assignments, or other additional income you might be eligible to receive.

Typical Federal Salaries

Your income increases quickly once you make it through training and payroll starts adding extras like educational incentive pay and advanced certification pay to your paycheck. Even if you are not eligible for those extras, your base pay will rise quickly after academy training and/or probationary periods. For example, the

Las Vegas, Nevada
Population: over one million (not including over 30 million annual visitors)

Las Vegas Metropolitan Police Department (merged with Clark County Sheriff's Dept. in 1973)
Number of commissioned officers: about 1,500
Base entry Level pay: $34,368/year

Austin, Texas
Population: over one million

Austin Police Department
Number of officers: over 1,000
Base entry level pay: $25,305/year

Phoenix, Arizona
Population: almost 3 million

Phoenix Police Department
Number of officers: about 2,100
Base entry level pay: $30,129

Atlanta, Georgia
Population: over 3.5 million

Atlanta Police Department
Number of officers: over 2,300
Base entry level pay: $22,803

Portland, Oregon
Population: over 2 million

Portland Police Department
Number of officers: almost 1,000
Base entry level pay: $30,300

Orlando, Florida
Population: almost 1.5 million

Orlando Police Department
Number of officers: over 600
Base entry level pay: $28,200

Denver, Colorado
Population: over 2 million

Denver Police Department
Number of officers: over 1,400
Base entry level pay: $31,512

West Palm Beach, Florida
Population: about 1 million

Palm Beach Police Department
Number of officers: over 70
Base entry level pay: $31,637 to $48,483 (based on experience)

starting pay with the Las Vegas Metro Police is $34,368. After training is completed (up to 20 weeks), your base pay will automatically rise to $36,660.

Federal employment might be more your speed; if so, we've provided the figures from Uncle Sam. Exact payment information is usually included on job announcements for specific jobs when posted by the agency looking for recruits. The chart below gives you an idea of what to expect for basic pay in 1998 for most federal law enforcement agencies. Each pay grade has 10 "steps," which we did not include here in the interest of keeping this issue simple. The Office of Personnel Management (OPM) can provide detailed pay charts at your request, and you'll see detailed information on how to contact them in chapter two.

General Schedule Pay

GS-1	$12,960	GS-6	$22,258	GS-11	$36,609
GS-2	14,571	GS-7	24,734	GS-12	43,876
GS-3	15,899	GS-8	27,393	GS-13	52,176
GS-4	17,848	GS-9	30,257	GS-14	61,656
GS-5	19,969	GS-10	33,320	GS-15	72,525

Your base pay is adjusted after training when you receive your first assignment. After relocating, pay rates in the U.S. can be adjusted anywhere from 5.6% to 12% higher than what you see in the chart. For example, say you've just been hired as a Special Agent with the FBI at pay grade GS-10, which is $33,320 a year. After training, your first assignment is Atlanta, Georgia. Your pay, according to the 1998 Salary Table published by the OPM, should climb to $36,559 because this area has a 6.18% locality payment. If you are assigned outside of the continental U.S., your base pay should be 10% to 25% higher.

It gets better. If you have skills that Uncle Sam has been having a hard time finding, you may also be offered a higher starting salary. For instance, some agencies start recruits with experience in the scientific, medical, and technical fields at a higher rate of pay. While we're on the subject of money, take a moment to check out the basic pay you can expect from some federal law enforcement jobs.

Entry Level Basic Pay by Occupation

Occupation	Starting Salary
FBI Special Agent	$33,320
U.S. Secret Service Special Agent	$19,969; $24,734; or $30,257*
U.S. Secret Service Uniformed Division Officer	$30,952
ATF Special Agent	$19,969 or $24,734*
Bureau of Prisons, Correctional Officer	$19,969 or $22,258*

*rate offered depends on your qualifications

THE RISKS

Law enforcement is not without risks. The injury rate among law enforcement officers is higher than in many other occupations, and for obvious reasons. How many bankers do you know who start their work weeks out with a high-speed car chase or end them taking drugs away from people who don't want to give them up? And even when law enforcement professionals aren't directly in harm's way, they often have to perform duties that are difficult or disturbing, such as dealing with bloody accident scenes or interviewing a victim of sexual assault. Dr. Rick Bradstreet, a police psychiatrist for over 19 years, suggests checking out the law enforcement career you want before diving in head first.

> Police work isn't the same as deputy sheriff's work, and deputy's work is not like DPS (state troopers) work. Go ride with officers in the area that you want to work. Get exposed to the work and talk to people about the real ups and downs. We've had people quit after seeing fatal auto accidents—one cadet saw a bloody bar fight and quit. They weren't exposed enough to the work to see that this isn't the job they wanted.

If risk isn't enough of a problem, there's its constant partner, stress. Stress is a part of life in law enforcement. It comes from coping with everything from angry motorists to nasty weather; from dealing with citizens who believe that all law enforcement officials are corrupt or racist, to dealing with the stress of not knowing what's going to happen next during a shift. And since cops, deputies, and federal agents are all human, there's a tendency to forget to leave the problems at work, which can sometimes lead to trouble with family relationships.

No, this isn't the fun part of thinking about a career in law enforcement. It's the reality, though, and you must have both feet firmly on the ground when you consider this career. Remember, too, that law enforcement takes care of its own— you'll get help and support from your partners and your agency if you have the maturity to ask for it when you need it.

THE DAY-TO-DAY

No matter what uniform or business suit you end up wearing with your badge, your equipment will have to include a pretty good sense of humor about a few basic precepts:

1. Everyone starts at the bottom—unless your department is so small that you are the only officer or agent!
2. The 40-hour work week is mostly an urban myth.
3. What most people call "Tuesday" or "Wednesday" you'll probably refer to as your "Saturday" or "Sunday."

The truth is, if you work in law enforcement you'll generally work rotating shifts, with rotating days off; you'll work nights, weekends, and holidays; and overtime pay is so likely you might as well add a column for it in your monthly household budget. These concerns can go in the Plus or Minus column—it all depends on how you look at it.

ABILITIES AND PERSONALITY TRAITS

So, have you asked yourself the hardest question of all: "Do I have what it takes to do the job?" Taking the Police Officer Suitability Test at the end of this chapter gave you a pretty good idea, but there's more.

You need to be strong—in more ways than one. You have to be physically strong, staying in excellent shape and being ready to run, jump, push, and pull when the time comes. Then there's strength of character and emotional stability, both crucial characteristics of a good law enforcement professional. In this line of work you must also have a highly-developed sense of responsibility and respect for authority. You'll need to be fair and open-minded, honest, even-tempered, tactful, quick-thinking, disciplined, and self-confident. And you *must* be able to make decisions independently, cope with high levels of stress, and exercise sound judgment.

You also have to be good at handling people; law enforcement is all about *people*—their actions and their reactions. You'll serve citizens who have different beliefs and who come from different backgrounds, of all races, religions, gender, sexual preference, age, and socioeconomic levels. No matter what form your private beliefs may take, you must treat all people equally and fairly under the law. Sheriff Don Farley, of the Rockingham County Sheriff's Office in Virginia, believes:

> Being an officer is much like being an umpire in a game. No matter
> what decision you make, someone is going to be upset. An officer
> must be able to interpret the law so that the people involved have an
> understanding about the action you have taken.

Though it may seem otherwise, you don't have to walk on water to get a law enforcement job, but if you *do* happen to have that skill, you're a shoo-in for first place on the hiring list! Everyone knows you are human, but you *will* be held to a higher standard because of the nature of the job.

To be successful you'll also need the following skills:

- *Good oral and written communication skills.* Law enforcement involves constant communication, whether it's with fellow officers, dispatchers, victims, witnesses, or suspects. You have to be able to express yourself in an appropriate, effective manner. The ability to write clearly and concisely is also important since you'll be writing reports that may become legal evidence in a court case.

- *Good observation skills.* If you aren't the type of person who notices what people are wearing or what's happening around you, it's best that you become one now! Your ability to notice and remember telling details can make conducting an investigation either a nightmare or a breeze. It's especially useful when you sit down to write your report and when you testify in court cases. It's the skill you need most to alert you to suspicious behavior.

- *Good memory.* A good memory is an essential law enforcement skill. It's important to know what kind of memory you have and to work on your memorization weaknesses. Some people remember names well, but can't put them with the right faces. Others forget names quickly, but know exactly when, where, and why they met the person whose name they've forgotten. If you don't think you have a good memory, then there's no time like the present to develop one! The key to a good memory is practice, practice, practice.

THE HIRING PROCESS

In order to be hired by a law enforcement agency you'll have to go through a selection process that can take anywhere from several months to a year or more. Why such a long and complicated process? Because law enforcement work—as police officer, state trooper, federal agent, or corrections officer—is tough. Whether you're patrolling a beat, the highways, or a cell block, you need a lot of positive character traits, life experience, and skills, and the agency you want to work for needs to know that you are qualified.

In most areas, many more people apply for law enforcement positions than can ever be accepted. For instance, thousands of applicants applied to the Portland Police Department in 1997, but only a hundred or so made the grade. The hiring process involves a series of steps that must be passed before an agency can put someone on its eligibility list; a large percentage of people who apply fail one or more of these steps.

The Exam Announcement

Here's the starting line for you: watching for special announcements from the agency for which you want to work. Don't rely on the "Help Wanted" section of your local newspaper to let you know when the Feds are hiring, or about a local department's openings for that matter. Most city, county, state, and federal agencies start looking for recruits by contacting their personnel departments, by placing notices on Home Pages on the World Wide Web, and by alerting their respective recruiting departments that the search is on. Your job is to contact these sites and people as often as is necessary to keep up with what's going on. If you have friends on the force, ask them to keep their ears to the ground for information, but don't rely *solely* on them.

The announcement will outline the basic qualifications for the position and, usually, the steps you'll have to go through in the selection process. If an entrance exam is part of the process, you'll likely see a date, time, and location for the exam, along with a phone number for whom to contact for more information. Get a written copy of the announcement from the department in which you want to work. Some agencies, though not many, keep an ongoing notification list so that they can drop you a postcard when the next exam is to be given. If exams are held frequently, you will sometimes be told to simply show up at the exam site on a given day of the week or month. In those cases, you usually get more information about the job and the selection process once you pass the written exam. *Read these announcements carefully* because you don't want to show up at the testing location at 9 a.m. to hear that the test started at 8:30.

If you call the agency to ask about an exam announcement or application, the person who answers the phone may conduct a brief prescreening to make sure that you meet the basic qualifications as to age, education, and so on. If this happens, keep your answers brief and *polite*. Please don't launch into your life story or complain to the person about their department's hiring process. The moment you make contact with an agency you begin establishing a reputation with them. The impression you leave on the phone may be the one that follows you through the entire process.

Speaking of phones, no matter where you are in the application process, if agency personnel call you for any reason and ask that you return their call, do so as quickly as you can. As one busy background investigator in Texas put it:

Don't make me call you three or four times! If I have to keep hunting you down to get the information I need, I will assume you aren't all that interested in a job with our department. And that means you may not be in our process for long.

The Application

Often the first step in the process of becoming a law enforcement officer is filling out an application. Depending on the employer, this application can be anywhere from one to 20 pages long. The initial paperwork will usually be screened to determine whether or not you meet the minimum hiring qualifications. You may be asked to fill out an application to take the written test, with a more detailed application to come later if you pass.

A Note About Resumes

Before you pay a professional resume writer half of next month's salary for a spiffy looking layout, you might want to check on whether or not the department even wants it. Many police, state police, sheriff's departments, and corrections agencies do not accept resumes. On the other hand, many federal agencies *do*, and they ask for them to follow specific formats. (The Office of Personnel Management has a resume format on hand that you can have sent to you, or you can use the on-line resume format on their Web page.) Check the job announcement closely to see what is required. If a resume is not required, save your time, energy, and money for the rest of the process!

The Written Exam

Most agencies give written exams as the next step in the application process, though in some cases a background interview may come first. (By putting the background interview first, agencies save themselves the expense of testing applicants who don't meet the basic qualifications.) As a rule, if you don't pass the test, you are out of the process. If you do, your score may be used to rank you on the eligibility list. In some cases, your score alone will determine your rank, while in others it's combined with physical agility, oral interview scores, and/or other testing results. The exam announcement will usually let you know how the ranking works.

Most written exams simply test basic skills and aptitudes: your reading comprehension, your writing ability, your ability to follow directions, your judgment and reasoning skills, and sometimes your memory or your math skills. On the federal level, you may be asked to take a test like the Treasury Enforcement Agent (TEA) exam. The TEA exam is a written examination that tests your judgment, logic, planning, and communication skills. Not all federal positions require it, but many agencies, such as the ATF, do.

Before giving you the exam, some agencies require that you study written material (study guides) in advance and then answer questions during the exam based on the study guide. Some of these study guides have to do with the law and police or corrections procedures, or they may contain photos and drawings for you to memorize.

Exams *are* nerve wracking, but they're given for good reasons. Departments need officers and agents who can read, understand, and make decisions based on complex written materials such as laws, policy handbooks, and regulations. You can't do the job without being able to write incident reports, affidavits, and other documents that are clear and correct for court or other formal legal proceedings. And you'll need sound mathematical skills for such basic tasks as adding up the value of stolen goods or calculating the street price of a kilo of cocaine confiscated in a drug raid. Entrance exams test for these basic skills.

As for format, most exams are multiple-choice tests like you were given in high school or college. You'll get an exam book and an answer sheet on which you'll have to fill in circles or squares with a number-two pencil. A few agencies, particularly municipal police departments, will also have you write an essay or a mock police report. Applicants are generally notified in writing about the results of the exam. Some agencies grade tests with scanners and can tell you immediately what your score is, although it's rare for you to find out your ranking until everyone's test has been graded; it's more common for you to get your results through the mail. After you've passed the written exam, the next step is usually the physical agility test.

The Physical Agility Test

Most agencies, from corrections to police departments, put applicants through their paces with an agility test. Some are complicated, some are not. For example, applicants with the Phoenix Police Department (AZ) are asked to scale a six-foot block wall, and do a 1.5 mile run, sit-ups, and bench press. Applicants are expected to perform the events according to their age, sex, and body weight ratio (for the bench press). On the other end of the spectrum, the Austin Police Department (TX) has a physical ability test consisting of a timed obstacle course 440 yards in length. The course is designed to simulate a foot pursuit and consists of 17 separate components, ending with the applicant dragging a 165-pound dummy 15 feet. No matter whose test you take, you can expect a fair amount of running, some lifting or other upper-body strength requirements, and often a test of hand strength that helps to determine whether you'll be able to handle a gun.

Sounds tough? It can be, but for the most part, the agility test is designed to find out whether you're in good enough shape to do well in the physical training part of the academy. The bottom line is, the better prepared you are physically, the better off you'll be during academy training. Most agencies will be happy to give you a detailed description of their agility requirements. There's more detailed information on physical agility testing in chapter six.

The Personal History Statement and Background Investigation

As the hiring agency more seriously considers your application, investigators will begin looking into your past and present circumstances, starting with the application form or with paperwork that is also called the personal history statement. Some agencies ask that you fill out this paperwork before you get to any of the other stages in the hiring process. Others prefer to wait until after the written exam and the agility test. Whenever you do it, it's safe to say that investigators can't begin until this crucial documentation is in their hands.

You'll most likely start by filling out the personal history form. Assume that everything you say will be double-checked by a trained, experienced investigator. You'll be asked where you were born, where you've lived, where you've gone to school (including elementary school), what you've studied, where you've worked and what duties you performed, what organizations you've belonged to. . . . You get the picture. Your whole life will be laid out on paper. You'll supply names of teachers, employers, neighbors, and relatives, as well as the names of several people who can attest to your character and fitness to become a law enforcement officer. Eventually, your phone will ring and an investigator with your dream agency will be on the other end telling you it's time to get started on your background check.

Investigators won't take your word for anything! Your information will be verified and all the facts checked out. If you write down that you were in the Army for three years and then got out with an honorable discharge, they'll contact the army to find out if this is true—and they'll interview your former superiors and peers while they're at it! They'll ask questions about how well you deal with problems, with stress, with people, and with the public. They'll find out how you meet your financial and personal obligations and they'll find out anything that might affect your eligibility for the law enforcement position of your dreams. When the investigator is finished, he or she will have a pretty complete picture of what kind of person you are. There's more about the strategy behind writing a successful personal history statement in chapter six.

Federal agencies who go through the OPM to hire their employees are just as serious about their applications as other law enforcement agencies. They expect your paperwork to be carefully filled out and their directions followed to a "T." For example, the general information section of the OPM's Optional Application for Federal Employment states:

> You may apply for most Federal jobs with a resume, this Optional Application for Federal Employment, or other written format. If your resume or application does not provide all in the information requested on this form and in the job vacancy announcement, you may lose consideration for a job. Type or print clearly in dark ink. Help speed the selection process by keeping your application brief and sending only the requested information. . . .

The OPM handles thousands of applications for federal employment, and you can bet they don't have much patience for sloppy, incomplete paperwork. There are too many qualified people competing for your job for you to take a chance with this part of the process.

The decision whether or not to hire you is going to come mostly as a result of what you put down in the personal history statement, and of what investigators find out about you. You may not see the results of your background check reflected in your rank on the eligibility list, but your rank won't matter much if you can't pass the background check. This is where the hiring agency checks not only your experience and education, but also—and most importantly—your character. Do you have the integrity, the honesty, the ability to commit, the personal stamina, and the respect for authority that a law enforcement officer must have? Rest assured that local, state, and federal agencies will go to a lot of trouble and expense to find out the answer.

Polygraph Testing

Some agencies use polygraph testing as part of their hiring process, and some don't. And some agencies who don't require it as a routine part of their investigation will reserve the right to use it if questions arise during your background check.

Though some people call the polygraph machine a "lie detector," there really is no such thing. What the polygraph detects is changes in heart and respiratory rates, blood pressure, and galvanic skin resistance (how much you're perspiring). A cuff like the one your doctor uses to take your blood pressure will be wrapped around your arm. Rubber tubes wrapped around your trunk will measure your breathing, and clips on your fingers or palm will measure skin response. The theory is that people who are consciously lying get nervous and are betrayed by their involuntary bodily responses.

Don't worry about flunking the test because of nervousness. You can't help but be a little anxious about this experience, but the polygraph examiner will explain the whole process to you. The examiner will ask you a series of questions to establish a baseline both for when you're telling the truth and for when you're not. For instance, the examiner might tell you to answer "no" to every question asked and then ask you whether your name is George (if it isn't) and whether you drove to the examination today (if you did).

All questions in a polygraph exam have to be in yes-or-no form. You will be told in advance what every question will be. Some questions will be easy lobs, like "Are you wearing sneakers?" The questions that really count will be the ones that relate to your fitness to be a law enforcement officer. You probably will have been over any problematic areas with the background investigator or other interviewers before, so just tell the truth and try to relax.

Oral Interviews and Selection Boards

So, you think the only time for sweating is during the physical agility course? Not so. There's nothing like a face-to-face interview to ruin a crisp ironing job! Every law enforcement position you apply for will have some kind of interview, whether it's a one-on-one chat with your background investigator to talk about your application or a full-blown oral interview board. Your safest bet is to expect to do a lot of talking during your application process. Border Patrol Agent Jeremy Farner remembers a little of his oral board interview:

> I had two people on my board, I think. It was very difficult, very stressful. They were very "pushy" for their answers and second-guessed everything I said.

Most agencies put their applicants through an oral board, even if the panel is staffed by only two people, like in Jeremy's case. An oral board is usually made up of two to five people who are either civilians or sworn officers. There's usually some variety in the makeup of the board to allow for different perspectives. The board's job is to assess your interpersonal skills, communication skills, judgment and decision-making abilities, respect for diversity, and your adaptability. Quite a task, especially when you consider that most interviews last only an hour or two.

The way the interview is conducted depends on the department. You may be asked a few questions similar to those you've experienced on civilian employment interviews: Why do you want this job? Why do you want to work for this agency? You will also be asked questions resulting from the background investigation. Dr. Rick Bradstreet estimates that he has sat on thousands of interview boards during his career as a police psychologist. When asked what the top three things an applicant can do *wrong* in an oral interview are, he replies:

> Number one is to get indignant about the questions that are being asked; number two is to give an answer to a question and then defend it to the death because they fear they'll look wishy-washy if they change it; and number three is to give vague responses to questions to try not to commit to an answer.

You may also be presented with hypothetical situations. A board member may simply describe a situation and then ask you what you would do, or one or more board members may role-play the situation, asking you to play the part of an officer. You may even watch a video that the board members will question you about at the end.

The trend is for more local and state-level agencies to put standardized questions on their oral boards. They ask each candidate the same questions and when the interview is over the board rates each candidate on a set scale. These standardized questions help the interviewers to reach a more objective conclusion about the candidates they have seen. These scores are usually added in to the other tests that make up your eligibility ranking.

The Psych Exam

At least you don't have to worry about studying before taking *this* exam. Although some people are offended by the mere thought of having to undergo a psychological examination, it's not an insult. Law enforcement work is one of the most stressful occupations in the world and it's in your best interest *and* that of your future employers' to weed out applicants who are unsuited for the job. While no one can guarantee that a given individual won't crack in a stressful situation, law enforcement agencies need to find those applicants with underlying instabilities, choosing only those who will be able to deal with the job in healthy ways. The evaluation is also used to give agencies a little insight into your personality, your habits, and other factors. You may encounter oral evaluations, written ones like the Minnesota Multiphasic Personality Inventory (MMPI), or a combination of both.

When taking an exam like the MMPI, the idea is to relax, answer honestly, and not give answers that you think will present you *only* in the best light. Dr. Bradstreet's advice for both written psychological exams and oral exams is:

> Applicants try to make themselves appear to walk on water by answering all of the questions to appear the most virtuous. The idea of trying to look so good is not a good idea. People who are candid about their strengths and weaknesses do the best.

Oral psychological interviews are usually conducted by a psychologist or psychiatrist employed by, or contracting with, the hiring agency. This person may ask you questions about your schooling, jobs, habits, hobbies, and family relationships. Since there's such a broad range of things you could be asked about, there's really no way to prepare. In fact, the psychologist may be more interested in the way you answer—whether you come across as open, forthright, and honest—than in the answers themselves.

The Medical Examination

This part of the process will usually come at the end, after a conditional offer of employment. The exam itself is nothing unusual; it will be just like any other thorough physical exam. The doctor may be on the staff of the hiring agency or someone outside of the department with his or her own private practice. Your blood pressure, temperature, weight, etc. will be measured; your heart and lungs will be listened to and your limbs examined. The doctor will ask you to "say ahhhh," peer into your eyes, ears, nose—you know the drill. You'll also have to donate a little blood and urine to the cause. Because some of these tests have to be sent out to a lab, you won't know the results of the physical exam right away. You'll be notified as soon as the test results are known.

Drug Screening

Drug screening is usually conducted at the same time the medical exam is administered, but can be done earlier in the process. Use of illegal drugs, of course, will get you booted right out of the process. If the test comes back positive because of a prescription drug you used, the department can ask you about it, but cannot use the condition for which the drug is prescribed to reject you, thanks to the Americans with Disabilities Act (ADA).

THE JOB

So far, you have a pretty good idea of what the general hiring process is like for most law enforcement agencies, and you know that no two hiring processes are alike. Now it's time to look at the jobs themselves, starting with local and state positions.

Police Officer

Everyone knows what a cop does, right? Probably—to a certain extent. If you've ever been on the receiving end of a traffic ticket then you know of at least one duty they perform. But that's an awfully narrow view of what a police officer does, and "narrow" is not a word you should use in connection with *this* job.

If you like variety you'll be well suited for police work. This is especially true for that first year on the force, the time when you are being exposed to as many different aspects of the job as humanly possible. With police work, you'll never be absolutely certain how your day at the "office" may turn out. Your shift may start out with a bang when your first call propels you down an alley after a robbery suspect, and it may end with the tedious task of lifting a thumbprint from the rear view mirror of a stolen car. You can rest assured that no matter what you do, you'll write reports galore at the end of the shift.

Realistically, you must expect to start at the bottom when you consider joining a police force of any size. If your main interest is in becoming a detective, you'll get there eventually, but not before you get the "street smarts" that only experience will provide. Chances are, your first assignment will be to the patrol division.

Patrol officers do exactly what their title implies: patrol a designated area, usually by car or on foot, and in some cases by motorcycle, bicycle, or horseback. You may work alone or with a partner, depending on the nature of your assignment and the size of the police force. Typically, you'll work 40-hour weeks on rotating shifts, and that doesn't include overtime or required court appearances. In some cases you may be offered the chance to work an extra shift, depending on the needs of the department.

Some of the duties of a patrol officer include:

- traffic control
- crowd control
- response to 911 calls
- fingerprinting
- securing the scene of a crime
- interviewing witnesses, victims, and suspects
- handling domestic disturbances
- making traffic stops
- subduing and arresting suspects

Qualifications

Although requirements for becoming a police officer vary among police departments, typically you must be a U.S. citizen between the ages of 18 and 29 at the time of appointment. Other possible requirements include:

- a valid driver's license and a good driving record
- a high school diploma or GED
- some college education (may be required or merely preferred)
- residency in the city or county in which you apply
- no felony convictions

There will be more, though that list will give you an idea of the basics. Some departments will ask that you have some college hours, and others will want you to have an associate degree or higher. Some will allow a misdemeanor record, according to what crimes were committed, and others will ask for near perfection. This is all for a good reason: you will be asked to safeguard the lives and property of citizens, to protect every citizen's constitutional rights, and to enforce the law fairly—not a list of tasks for the average person. Once again, if it seems that you are being held to a higher standard, there's no mistake about it—you are!

Selection Process

Law enforcement agencies across the U.S. are getting a lot pickier about who they hire and how they go about doing it, understandably. Situations like the Rodney King case in California and similar cases across the nation have caused departments to become more concerned about departmental liability when it comes to the actions of their officers. What does that mean to you? It simply means you should expect to jump through a few more hoops than your predecessors. For example, most agencies will ask that you undergo some, if not all, of the following:

- written examination
- physical agility testing
- psychological testing
- polygraph examination
- background investigation
- oral interview sessions

Training

After you make it through the selection process and you've been offered the job, your next goals are to pass the training program in the academy and to make it through the probationary period. If your agency puts you through an academy program, you'll learn all the skills you need to make it as a police officer. If the agency you go to work for does *not* have an academy, you may be sponsored by your police department (meaning they pay the bills for your training) and sent to a regional academy. For example, the Plymouth Regional Police Academy in Massachusetts provides training for basic municipal police recruits for municipal police departments in the southeast part of the state, in Cape Cod, and in the Islands.

The exact curriculum and number of hours of instruction may vary among different police academies, but they usually address similar subject and skill areas. Your classroom training may start with an overview of the U.S. criminal justice system, for example. This may cover both law enforcement agencies and the courts, and probably includes a look at both the history of policing and modern policing strategies.

You'll learn about constitutional law and penal, civil, juvenile, and vehicle/traffic law. You'll also receive plenty of instruction about police discretionary powers and the use of physical force. The more personal side of policing—interacting with the public, handling the pressures of the job, and so forth—will be handled under the classroom topics of community relations and public service, police ethics, and stress management.

Skills training is another major portion of a police academy course. You'll become adept in the use of firearms and other police weapons and equipment such as the night stick and handcuffs. Physical fitness training will become a priority in your life. You'll be glad you're getting in top-notch shape when you get to the self-defense, physical restraint, and arrest techniques training.

In recent years, community colleges in many states have started offering police academy training, sometimes called "open enrollment academies." The subjects and training offered in these settings are the same as what you'd find in the departmental police departments, if not more. Students may be required to take college courses in areas such as English composition or basic criminal law as prerequisites to the academy course. The main differences, however, are that you'll be taking on the financial responsibility yourself, and that you don't necessarily have to have a job in law enforcement waiting for you upon graduation. Usually the bill includes registration and administrative fees, plus costs for books, equipment, weapons, uniforms and other gear. (Costs vary by institution, but plan on a total of roughly $1,400 to $1,800.) What you get in return is certification as a police officer and proof that you've got what it takes to do the job. This is exactly what you'll need for those instances when you apply to a department that requires you to be certified before they will hire you. Most agencies will make it clear to you whether or not you should already be certified, but be sure you know before you get too invested in the process! To find out about these programs, contact the admissions director of the community college nearest to you. Your local police department can point you in the right direction as well.

Your training is not really considered to be complete by most departments without a bit of OJT (on-the-job-training) by a field training officer. Field training is conducted after you've finished the police academy program, though some academies consider it to be the final phase of their program. On the whole, departments include the time you spend in field training as part of the probationary employment period for new officers. Its main purpose is to provide practical experience in policing. When you're participating in either formal field training programs or supervised on-the-job training, departments have the chance to gauge your technical skills, your knowledge of the law, and the procedures you learned in the classroom, and how you interact with the public. This is where the department gets a chance to see if their time, money, and training has paid off. Field training officers who do not feel comfortable with your knowledge and performance can recommend that the department either retrain you or fire you.

Deputy Sheriff

A deputy sheriff is a law enforcement officer hired by the sheriff's office in a county. The position of deputy is often an "at will" position, meaning that deputies serve at the will of the sheriff. The sheriff, on the other hand, is usually an elected official and serves at the will of the voter.

Applying for the Job

To find out about the latest job openings in your community, call your local police department's non-emergency number. Also, check out Web sites like *www.policenet.com* and *www.officer.com* for detailed information about departments all over the U.S. Remember that list of the nation's fastest growing municipal police departments at the beginning of the chapter? Well, here are the addresses to contact them:

Las Vegas Metropolitan Police
Department
(merged with Clark County)
Personnel Department
(702) 229-3497

Austin Police Department
Recruiting Section
2785 E. 7th Street
Austin, TX 78702
(512) 305-4000

Phoenix Police Department
Personnel Department, Application
Office
135 N. Second Avenue
Phoenix, AZ 85016
To have applications mailed, call:
(602) 262-6277

Orlando Police Department
Recruiting Section
100 S. Hughey Avenue
Orlando, FL 32801
(407) 246-2470

Palm Beach Police Department
Personnel Office
360 South County Road
Palm Beach, FL 33480
(561) 838-5450

Denver Police Department
Recruiting Section
1331 Cherokee Street
Denver, CO 80204
(303) 640-2575

Portland Police Department
Where to Apply in Person:
Portland Bureau of Personnel
Interim City Hall
1400 SW 5th Avenue, 10th floor
Where to Mail your Application:
Portland Bureau of Personnel
1220 SW 5th Avenue
Portland, OR 97204
(502) 823-4636

After being hired as a deputy sheriff, you'll patrol rural areas or places that aren't served by a local police department. Like police officers, you'll patrol an assigned area in a marked patrol car, investigate suspicious or criminal activity, and you'll have all the necessary powers of arrest, search, and seizure. Your main responsibilities, of course, are the protection of people and property. Some of your more specific job duties will include:

- crowd control
- writing citations for traffic violations on county roads
- emergency first aid for accident victims or victims of violent crime
- crime scene duties
    - fingerprinting
    - evidence procurement
    - crime scene security
    - witness, victim, and suspect interviews
- surveillance work
- undercover work
- service with SWAT units or other specialized details

You will usually work 40-hour weeks on rotating shifts, and you will put in extra hours from time to time. Don't be surprised when you are called in to testify in court about that homicide you worked last weekend, and be prepared to show up for extra duty when your supervisor calls. Whether you drive your cruiser alone or ride with a partner will depend on the size and needs of your department.

The sheriff's department is responsible for operating, maintaining, and staffing correctional facilities for the county. They also provide security for court houses and courtrooms. Consequently, you could find yourself:

- serving subpoenas, summonses, warrants and other court orders
- conducting evictions
- escorting prisoners to and from correction facilities
- extraditing fugitives from other jurisdictions

Qualifications

Different counties have different criteria for hiring deputy sheriffs. In most places, you must be between 21 and 29 years of age, be a U.S. citizen, and have a valid driver's license. You'll also need a high school diploma or a General Equivalency Degree (GED), and if not a completed degree, maybe some college hours.

Selection Process

You won't be surprised to hear that sheriff's departments all seem to have a different selection process. Some employers will ask that you pass a written exam, while others will only want to see the results of your background investigation and/or personal interview before they hire you. Larger departments will usually require that you go through a more stringent process involving some, if not all, of the following:

- written exams
- physical agility tests
- psychological testing
- physical exams
- polygraph testing
- background investigations
- oral interview boards

Training Involved

Training tends to vary even more than hiring requirements among different counties. Often the type and amount of training you have to complete depends on the size of the department and its budget. Smaller departments may opt for on-the-job training under close supervision by a superior officer, while larger departments may have formal training procedures lasting anywhere from six weeks to six months, followed by supervised on-the-job training. In any event, all officers are required to meet minimum training standards set forth by each state.

Applying for the Job

To find out about the latest job openings in your community, call your local County employment office. You can also read about departments across the country if you check out the Web site entitled "Internet Home of the National Sheriff's Association" at *www.sheriffs.org*.

To find out about deputy sheriff positions in the nation's fastest growing counties, check out the listing on the next page.

Travis County Sheriff's Department
1010 W. Lavaca Street, 2nd Floor
Austin, TX 78701
(512) 473-9000

Multnomah County Sheriff's Office
12240 NE Glisan
Portland, OR 97230
503) 255-3600
FAX: (503) 253-2663

Palm Beach County Sheriff's Office
3228 Gun Club Road
West Palm Beach, FL 33406-3001
(561) 688-3000

Denver County Sheriff's Office
Career Service Authority
110 16th Street, Suite 450
Denver, CO 80202
(303) 640-4301
Job Line: (303) 640-1234
FAX: (303) 640-2359
TDD: (303) 640-3057

Orange County Sheriff's Office
Human Resources
2450 W. 33rd Street
Orlando, FL 32839
Job Line: 407-836-4071

Las Vegas Metropolitan Police Department
(merged with Clark County)
Personnel Department
(702) 229-3497

Maricopa County Sheriff's Office
Maricopa County Human Resources Dept.
301 West Jefferson Street, Suite 200
Phoenix, AZ 85003-2113
Recorded Job Information:
(602) 506-3329
Teletypewriter (TT): (602) 506-1908
FAX: (602) 560-3313

State Police Officer

When stranded on the highway in the middle of nowhere, there's no more welcome sight than the red and blue lights of a highway patrol cruiser. Rescuing stranded motorists is not the only duty of a state trooper, however. Although his or her main responsibility is to ensure public safety on the state's roadways, a highway patrol officer's job is like that of a deputy or municipal police officer. They patrol their assigned areas, enforce traffic laws, deal with accidents and other emergencies, and provide safety programs for the public. In communities and counties that do not have a local police force or a large sheriff's department, state troopers are the primary law enforcement agents, investigating crimes such as burglary or assault.

Depending on what state you are in, state troopers go by different names: state trooper, highway patrol officer, state police officer, or state traffic officer. If you are lucky enough to join their ranks, you'll experience a camaraderie that will last a lifetime.

Some of the more specific duties of a state trooper are:

- observing and reporting public safety hazards, such as unsafe driving conditions or roadway obstacles
- investigating conditions and causes of accidents
- appearing in court as witnesses in traffic and criminal cases
- writing reports
- assisting law enforcement officers from other jurisdictions
- conducting driver exams
- monitoring violations of commercial vehicle weight laws
- arresting persons who are driving while intoxicated
- executing search and/or arrest warrants
- enforcing drug laws

Qualifications

Requirements for this position vary among the states, but usually you must be a U.S. citizen between 21 and 29 years of age at the time of appointment and a resident of the state in which you are applying. Other requirements include:

- a valid driver's license and a good driving record
- a high school diploma or GED
- at least 60 college hours (may be required or merely preferred)
- no felony convictions

Selection Process

Again, the selection process will vary. At the least, you should expect:

- written testing
- physical agility testing
- psychological testing
- polygraph examination
- drug screening
- background investigation
- medical examination

Applying for the Job

State police traditionally request that you contact the troop or district office nearest to your home town for recruiting information. Consult your phone book for the numbers in your community. You can also consult the contact list for corrections officer in this chapter for a listing of state job lines and personnel offices. And don't forget to check for links to state police sites on the Web site "Law Enforcement Sites on the Web" at *www.ih2000.net/ira/ira2.htm.*

Corrections Officer

Corrections is the fastest growing job in the law enforcement field. A big part of the reason is that law enforcement is putting more criminals in jail. The U.S. Department of Justice reports that by mid-year 1997, one in every 155 U.S. residents was behind bars. As of June 1996, the nation's prisons and jails held 1,725,842 men and women, an increase of more than 96,100 inmates since 1995. The get-tough-on-crime push of the past few years has meant more jails, prisons, and detention centers popping up across the country. All this translates to a higher demand for corrections officers.

Once you make it into the field of corrections as a corrections officer, your primary duty will be to guard and supervise prisoners confined to penal institutions. This basic role doesn't change from facility to facility, but your specific duties will, depending on the size and type of institution.

As a corrections officer, you might work in a small county or municipal jail where you'll have a general range of duties, or you may work in a large state or federal prison with more specialized duties. Regardless of which place you choose, it'll be up to you to maintain order, enforce the rules of the institution, ensure the safety of inmates and fellow officers, and prevent escape.

If you are an unarmed corrections officer, you'll be responsible for the direct supervision of inmates. You may be locked in a cell block alone, or with another officer, to watch 50 to 100 inmates. Here, your excellent communication skills will work to your advantage. You'll routinely search inmates and cells for weapons, drugs, or other illegal items. You'll supervise inmates while they work, exercise, eat, and bathe. You'll rattle doors, check locks, and inspect windows and bars to make sure that none of them have been tampered with and that all are functioning properly. And you'll be on constant alert for any signs of tension or disruptive conduct among inmates that could lead to fighting or riots.

The disciplinary role you'll play as a corrections officer is a crucial element of your job. You can't show favoritism in your dealings with inmates and you must be prepared to use the appropriate level of force to protect the inmates under your supervision. That may include anything from the use of your voice to hand-to-hand defensive tactics to the use of weapons.

You may have a choice between working indoors or outdoors. Inmates have to be supervised during outside exercise activities and officers must be stationed around the perimeters of the facility, so there is some variety of work enviroment available. Corrections officers usually work eight-hour shifts, five days a week, with rotating days off. Since security is a 24-hour occupation, be prepared to work late-night hours, weekends, and holidays until you get a little on-the-job seniority. There are usually overtime hours as well.

To get an in-depth idea of what life is like as a corrections officer, you might want to check out Daniel J. Bayse's book, *Working in Jails & Prisons*. This book is geared toward new corrections officers and corrections staff. You'll get a very detailed, realistic idea of what life is like inside a facility and what you'll be expected to do. Call the American Correctional Association at 1-800-222-5646 for more information about this book.

Qualifications

Most institutions ask that you be:

- a minimum of 18 to 21 years old
- a citizen of the U.S.
- a high school graduate, or the equivalent
- in good health
- a licensed driver

More and more institutions are looking for applicants with college educations, especially those who've studied psychology, criminal justice, police science, criminology, or similar subjects. A stable work history also wins big points with most hiring agencies.

Selection Process

The selection process may vary considerably among agencies, depending on whether you apply to the county, state, or federal system. Federal requirements are generally the most stringent. At the least, be prepared to pass the following:

- drug screening
- written or oral examinations
- background checks
- psychological examination

Training

When you're first hired as a corrections officer, you will be considered a probationary employee as you begin training. Federal, state, and local corrections departments use training guidelines set by certain professional organizations, including the American Correctional Association and the American Jail Association. What varies from institution to institution is whether you'll receive mostly on-the-job training or first go through a formal training program, such as an academy.

Corrections officers in federal prisons get their training through the Federal Bureau of Prisons at Glynco, Georgia. Within 60 days of being hired, you'll be required to complete 120 hours of specialized correctional instruction at Glynco. You need to have 200 hours of formal training within the first year of employment with the Feds. Once you are back home on the job, you'll be supervised by more experienced officers in an on-the-job training environment.

Corrections officers hired at the state and local level usually rely heavily on on-the-job training, though they are required to go through formal training courses mandated by the state. Many state facilities are in the process of developing formal training programs similar to the Federal Bureau of Prisons, and already have special training academies.

Training usually includes instruction on institution rules, regulations, and operations. You'll also get plenty of instruction on:

- constitutional law
- custody and security procedures
- fire and safety
- CPR training
- crisis intervention
- inmate behavior
- contraband control
- report writing
- firearms and hand-to-hand self-defense instruction
- physical fitness training

At all institutions—federal, state, and local—it's common for corrections officers to participate in formal training courses after being employed for some time. Generally, this in-service training is designed to teach officers new ideas and techniques or certain specialized skills, often for job advancement.

On-Line Corrections Connections

♦ **Federal Bureau of Prisons**—facts and research related to the federal prison system, including an overview of the organization and its regional offices and facilities. [URL: *http//www.usdoj.gov/bop/bop.html*]

♦ **International Association of Correctional Officers (IACO)**—home page of this non-profit organization that is dedicated to serving the professional advancement of correctional officers; includes information about becoming a member and/or subscribing to IACO publications. [URL: *http//www.acsp.uic.edu/iaco/about.htm*]

♦ **The Keeper's Voice**—on-line version of the quarterly newsletter published by the IACO, which offers articles about issues, trends and people working in the field of corrections. [URL: *http//www.acsp.uic.edu/iaco/kv1601tc.htm*]

♦ **Secure and Community Corrections**—a summary report that links to numerous sites specific to the prison system and the field of corrections, including a variety of research and other material with a "real world" view of prison life. [URL: *http//orion.alaska.edu/~afdsw/prison.html*]

♦ **Life in Prison**—a guided tour of two Oregon prisons (one medium, one maximum security) using text and photos to describe the facilities, the daily routine and the on-site manufacturing plants in which the inmates work. [URL: *http//www.teleport.com/~jailjean/tourpris.html*]

♦ **Cecil Greek's Criminal Justice Page**—a sizable list of on-line resources spanning the field of criminal justice, law enforcement and the legal system, with access to many sites relevant to corrections and the penal system. [URL: *http://www.stpt.usf.edu/~greek/cj.html*]

Applying for the Job

Start by checking out the list of addresses in the deputy sheriff section on page 20 for a few of the hottest growing areas in the U.S. You can find details on the Web by reveiwing "The Corrections Connection Network" at *www.corrections.com*. From that site you'll find other links to corrections-related sites. You can also find an exhaustive list of facilities in the directory entitled *Directory of Juvenile and Adult Correctional Departments*, published by the American Correctional Association. Call 1-800-222-5646 for more information. Additional state-level employment contacts for corrections positions are included on the next page.

Alaska Department of Corrections
State of Alaska Recruitment
Information Line
P.O. Box 112000
Juneau, AK 99811-2000
(907) 465-8910—Juneau
(907) 563-0200—Anchorage

Arizona Department of Corrections
ADC Staffing Unit
1645 West Jefferson, Mail Code 540
Phoenix, AZ 85007
To request application: (602) 542-5608

Colorado Department of Corrections
2862 S Circle Drive #400
Colorado Springs, CO 80906
(719) 579-9580
FAX: (719) 540-4955

Department of Public Safety
Personnel Management Office
919 Ala Moana Blvd., Rm. 117
Honolulu, Hawaii 96814
(808) 587-0936

Idaho Personnel Commission
700 West State Street
P.O. Box 83720
Boise, Idaho 83720-0066
(208) 334-2263
(800) 554-5627

Indiana Dept. of Correction
(800) 638-3960

Iowa Department of Personnel
Grimes State Office Building
East Fourteenth Street at Grand Avenue
Des Moines, IA 50319-0150
Job Line: (515) 281-5820
To request an application:
(515) 281-3087 (automated call process-
ing system)

Kentucky Department for Employment
Services
275 East Main Street
Frankfort, KY 40621
(502) 564-5331

Department of Labor Job Service
Bureau of Employment Services
55 State House Station
Augusta, ME 04333-0055
(207) 624-6390

Maryland Office of Human Resources
Recruitment Division, 301 W.
Preston Street
Baltimore, MD 21201
(800) 705-3493

Massachusetts Department of Correction
The Department of Correction
Recruitment Office
(617) 727-3300 ext. 195.
State of Oregon Job Line
(503) 225-5555 Ext. 7777

Florida Department of Corrections
(888) 610-0603

State of Utah Job Hotline
(801) 538-3118

THE POLICE OFFICER SUITABILITY TEST

Wanting to be a police officer is one thing; being suited for it is another. The following self-evaluation quiz can help you decide whether you and this career will make a good match. There is no one "type" of person who becomes a police officer. Cops are as varied as any other group of people in their personalities, experiences, and styles. At the same time, there are some attitudes and behaviors that predict success and satisfaction in this profession. They have nothing to do with your intelligence or ability; they simply reflect how you interact with other people and how you choose to approach the world.

These "suitability factors" were pulled from research literature and discussions with police psychologists and screeners across the country. The factors fall into five groups; each has 10 questions spaced throughout this test.

The LearningExpress Police Officer Suitability Test is not a formal psychological test. For one thing, it's not long enough; the MMPI (Minnesota Multiphasic Personality Inventory) test used in most psychological assessments has 11 times more items than you'll find here. For another, it does not focus on your general mental health.

Instead, the test should be viewed as an informal guide, a private tool to help you decide whether being a police officer would suit you, and whether you would enjoy it. It also provides the opportunity for greater self-understanding, which is beneficial no matter what you do for a living.

Directions

You'll need about 20 minutes to answer the 50 questions below. It's a good idea to do them all at one sitting—scoring and interpretation can be done later. For each question, consider how often the attitude or behavior applies to you. You have a choice between Never, Rarely, Sometimes, Often, and Always; put the number for your answer in the space after each question. For example, if the answer is "sometimes," the score for that item is 10; "always" gets a 40, etc. How they add up will be explained later. If you try to outsmart the test or figure out the "right" answers, you won't get an accurate picture. So just be honest.

PLEASE NOTE: Don't read the scoring sections before you answer the questions, or you'll defeat the whole purpose of the exercise!

How often do the following statements sound like you? Choose one answer for each statement.

NEVER	RARELY	SOMETIMES	OFTEN	ALWAYS
0	5	10	20	40

1. I like to know what's expected of me. _____

2. I am willing to admit my mistakes to other people. _____

3. Once I've made a decision, I stop thinking about it. _____

4. I can shrug off my fears about getting physically hurt. _____

5. I like to know what to expect. _____

6. It takes a lot to get me really angry. _____

7. My first impressions of people tend to be accurate. _____

8. I am aware of my stress level. _____

9. I like to tell other people what to do. _____

10. I enjoy working with others. _____

11. I trust my instincts. _____

12. I enjoy being teased. _____

13. I will spend as much time as it takes to settle a disagreement. _____

14. I feel comfortable in new social situations. _____

15. When I disagree with people, I let them know about it. _____

16. I'm in a good mood. _____

17. I'm comfortable making quick decisions when necessary. _____

18. Rules must be obeyed, even if you don't agree with them. _____

19. I like to say exactly what I mean. _____

20. I enjoy being with people. _____

21. I stay away from doing exciting things that I know are dangerous. _____

22. I don't mind when a boss tells me what to do._____

23. I enjoy solving puzzles. _____

24. The people I know consult me about their problems. _____

25. I am comfortable making my own decisions. _____

26. People know where I stand on things. _____

27. When I get stressed, I know how to make myself relax. _____

28. I have confidence in my own judgment. _____

29. I make my friends laugh. _____

30. When I make a promise, I keep it. _____

31. When I'm in a group, I tend to be the leader. _____

32. I can deal with sudden changes in my routine. _____

33. When I get into a fight, I can stop myself from losing control. _____

34. I am open to new facts that might change my mind. _____

35. I understand why I do the things I do. _____

36. I'm good at calming people down. _____

37. I can tell how people are feeling even when they don't say anything. _____

38. I take criticism without getting upset. _____

39. People follow my advice. _____

40. I pay attention to people's body language. _____

41. It's important for me to make a good impression. _____

42. I remember to show up on time. _____

43. When I meet new people, I try to understand them. _____

44. I avoid doing things on impulse. _____

45. Being respected is important to me. _____

46. People see me as a calm person. _____

47. It's more important for me to do a good job than to get praised for it.

_____

48. I make my decisions based on common sense. _____

49. I prefer to keep my feelings to myself when I'm with strangers. _____

50. I take responsibility for my own actions rather than blame others. _____

Scoring

Attitudes and behaviors can't be measured in units, like distance or weight. Besides, psychological categories tend to overlap. As a result, the numbers and dividing lines between score ranges are approximate, and numbers may vary about 20 points either way. If your score doesn't fall in the optimal range, it doesn't indicate a "failure"—only an area that needs focus.

It may help to share your test results with some of the people who are close to you. Very often, there are differences between how we see ourselves and how we actually come across to others.

GROUP 1—RISK

Add up scores for questions 4, 6, 12, 15, 21, 27, 33, 38, 44, and 46
TOTAL = _____

This group evaluates your tendency to be assertive and take risks. The ideal is in the middle, somewhere between timid and reckless: you should be willing to take risks, but not seek them out just for excitement. Being nervous, impulsive, and afraid of physical injury are all undesirable traits for a police officer. This group also reflects how well you take teasing and criticism, both of which you may encounter every day. And as you can imagine, it's also important for someone who carries a gun not to have a short fuse.

- A score between 360 and 400 is rather extreme, suggesting a kind of macho approach that could be dangerous in the field.
- If you score between 170 and 360, you are on the right track.

♦ If you score between 80 and 170, you may want to think about how comfortable you are with the idea of confrontation.

♦ A score between 0 and 80 indicates that the more dangerous and stressful aspects of the job might be difficult for you.

GROUP 2—CORE

Add up scores for questions 2, 8, 16, 19, 26, 30, 35, 42, 47, and 50
TOTAL = _____

This group reflects such basic traits as stability, reliability, and self-awareness. Can your fellow officers count on you to back them up and do your part? Are you secure enough to do your job without needing praise? Because, in the words of one police psychologist, "If you're hungry for praise, you will starve to death." The public will not always appreciate your efforts, and your supervisors and colleagues may be too busy or preoccupied to pat you on the back.

It is crucial to be able to admit your mistakes and take responsibility for your actions, to be confident without being arrogant or conceited, and to be straight-forward and direct in your communication. In a job where lives are at stake, the facts must be clear. Mood is also very important. While we all have good and bad days, someone who is depressed much of the time is not encouraged to pursue police work; depression affects one's judgment, energy level, and the ability to respond and communicate.

♦ If you score between 180 and 360, you're in the ballpark. 360+ may be unrealistic.

♦ A score of 100-180 indicates you should look at the questions again and re-evaluate your style of social interaction.

♦ Scores between 0 and 100 suggest you may not be ready for this job—yet.

GROUP 3—JUDGMENT

Add scores for questions 3, 7, 11, 17, 23, 28, 37, 40, 43, and 48
TOTAL = _____

This group reveals how you make decisions. Successful police officers are sensitive to unspoken messages, can detect and respond to other people's feelings, and make fair and accurate assessments of a situation, rather than being influenced by their own personal biases and needs. Once the decision to act is made, second-guessing can be dangerous. Police officers must make their best judgments in line with accepted practices, and then act upon these judgments without hesitancy or self-doubt. Finally, it's important to know and accept that you cannot change the world single-handedly. People who seek this career because they want to make a dramatic individual difference in human suffering are likely to be frustrated and disappointed.

- A score over 360 indicates you may be trying too hard.
- If you scored between 170 and 360, your style of making decisions, especially about people, fits with the desired police officer profile.
- Scores between 80 and 170 suggest that you think about how you make judgments and how much confidence you have in them.
- If you scored less than 170, making judgments may be a problem area for you.

GROUP 4—AUTHORITY

Add scores for questions 1, 10, 13, 18, 22, 25, 31, 34, 39, and 45

TOTAL = _____

This group contains the essential attributes of respect for rules and authority—including the "personal authority" of self-reliance and leadership—and the ability to resolve conflict and work with a team. Once again, a good balance is the key. Police officers must accept and communicate the value of structure and control without being rigid. And even though most decisions are made independently in the field, the authority of the supervisor and the law must be obeyed at all times. Anyone on a personal mission for justice or vengeance will not make a good police officer and is unlikely to make it through the screening process.

- A score between 160 and 360 indicates you have the desired attitude toward authority—both your own and that of your superior officers. Any higher is a bit extreme.
- If you scored between 100 and 160, you might think about whether a demanding leadership role is something you want every day.
- With scores between 0 and 100, ask yourself whether the required combination of structure and independence would be comfortable for you.

GROUP 5—STYLE

Add up scores for questions 5, 9, 14, 20, 24, 29, 32, 36, 41, and 49

TOTAL = ____

This is the personal style dimension, which describes how you come across to others. Moderation rules here as well: police officers should be seen as strong and capable, but not dramatic or heavy-handed; friendly, but not overly concerned with whether they are liked; patient, but not to the point of losing control of a situation. A good sense of humor is essential, not only in the field but among one's fellow officers. Flexibility is another valuable trait—especially given all the changes that can happen in one shift—but too much flexibility can be perceived as weakness.

- A score between 160 and 360 is optimal. Over 360 is trying too hard.
- Scores between 80 and 160 suggest that you compare your style with the above description and consider whether anything needs to be modified.
- If you scored between 0 and 80, you might think about the way you interact with others and whether you'd be happy in a job where people are the main focus.

Summary

The Police Officer Suitability Test reflects the fact that being a successful police officer requires moderation rather than extremes. Attitudes that are desirable in reasonable amounts can become a problem if they are too strong. For example, independence is a necessary trait, but too much of it creates a "Dirty Harry" type who takes the law into his or her own hands. Going outside accepted police procedure is a bad idea; worse, it can put other people's lives in jeopardy.

As one recruiter said, the ideal police officer is "low key and low maintenance." In fact, there's only one thing you can't have too much of, and that's common sense. With everything else, balance is the key. Keep this in mind as you look at your scores.

*This test was developed by Judith Schlesinger, Ph.D., a writer and psychologist whose background includes years of working with police officers in psychiatric crisis interventions.

THE INSIDE TRACK

Who:	Martina "Tina" Dominguez
What:	Uniformed Patrol Officer
Where:	Austin Police Department (APD) in Austin, Texas
How long:	Over three years
Degree:	Law enforcement academy

Insider's Advice

I guess I'd say make sure this job is what you want to do and then do it. Life is short. Don't get to where you say to yourself "What if I could have done that?"

Also, make sure you are in shape and work out! And don't do silly things—don't speed, don't get in trouble. Don't make the process harder than it has to be.

I like my job so much it's scary. I worked in an office for 11 1/2 years. Sometimes I drove home thinking "well, I just killed another tree, that's all I did today." But as a police officer, I think I'm able to do something that makes a difference—*really* makes a difference.

Insider's Take on the Future

If you go into a law enforcement position like mine, your typical day might be patrolling the streets alone in a patrol car, working 10-hour shifts, with three days off per week. When I get to work I check the BOLO list (be-on-the-lookout-for) to see what cars have been stolen recently. I make a list of them and then I go into show-up for about 10 to 15 minutes, and then we hit the street.

I handle whatever comes up. I usually make traffic stops, make DWI (Driving While Intoxicated) arrests, and drive around looking for things. On the weekends we handle a lot of loud noise calls from people complaining about college students partying all night. At the end of the shift I go back to the station, unload my car, and then take my laptop computer into the substation and download my reports into the computer. I print out a receipt for the reports and turn them into my supervisor.

The thing I like most about my job is making DWI arrests, because I can get [drunk drivers] off the streets. That makes me feel good.

CHAPTER | 2

This chapter will introduce you to the law enforcement hiring process at the federal level, starting with a detailed look at the Office of Personnel Management. You'll see descriptions of the most popular federal jobs and the duties these positions require. Details about the hiring process, minimum requirements, and testing procedures for all of these positions are also included.

FEDERAL JOBS IN LAW ENFORCEMENT

A law enforcement position with the U.S. Government is a highly appealing proposition. And the federal hiring machine has been busy, busy, busy, according to information from the U.S. Department of Justice. As of June 1996, 74,500 full-time law enforcement officers work for the federal government, up about 6% from 1993, the last time the Bureau of Justice Statistics conducted a head count.

Federal agencies will still be in hire-mode for a while, fortunately for you. Once you are hired by one of these agencies, you'll get general law enforcement training, most likely through the Federal Law Enforcement Training Center in Glynco, Georgia, as well as specialized training specifically geared for your new line of work. Whatever its mission or jurisdiction, these agencies frequently help each other out with criminal investigations or special projects, including emergency situations.

Largest Employers of Federal Officers Who Are Authorized to Carry Firearms and Make Arrests

AGENCY	NUMBER OF OFFICERS
Immigration and Naturalization Service	12,403
Bureau of Prisons	11,239
FBI	10,389
U.S. Customs Service	9,749
U.S. Secret Service	3,185

Source: U.S. Department of Justice Bureau of Justice Statistics—June 1996

Information about minimum requirements, applications, and testing appears later in this chapter, along with some federal job descriptions, but first, you need a bit of general information about the federal hiring process.

Office of Personnel Management

Some federal agencies have the authority to test and hire applicants directly, while others work through the Office of Personnel Management (OPM). When this is the case, the OPM typically accepts applications for employment with a specific federal agency; administers the appropriate written tests; and then submits an eligibility list of qualified candidates to the agency for consideration. For example, if you want a job with The Bureau of Alcohol, Tobacco and Firearms (ATF), you'll have to wait until you see a specific vacancy announcement posted through the OPM, then go through the office to start the application process. (If you already work for a federal agency, you may be able to apply directly to another agency rather than go through the OPM.)

The OPM operates Federal Job Information/Testing Centers in major metropolitan areas across the county. When written tests are required by an agency that works through the OPM, these tests generally will be given at these centers.

You can find out about current job openings and request the application forms you'll need when you contact the OPM. Not only will they provide access to federal job listings *and* some local and state government listings, they also have private sector listings. This is where you'll find the most up-to-date information, because it's updated daily and is available every day, 24 hours a day. It doesn't get much easier than this.

There are several ways to get information from OPM. By telephone, dial 912-757-3000 (TDD Service at 912-744-2299) to reach the OPM's Career America Connection. What you'll find here includes current federal job opportunities, salary and employee benefits information, and special recruitment information. While you have them on the line, leave a recorded request for the OPM to mail you an application package, specific forms, or other employment-related material. They'll fax or mail your order. If you'd like a complete listing of local telephone numbers for Career America Connection, ask them for fact sheet EI-42 entitled *Federal Employment Information Sources.*

If you'd rather use your computer, you can get the same information by using the OPM's Federal Job Opportunities Bulletin Board (FJOB) by having your modem dial 912-757-3100. Don't dial this number without a computer! Computer-savvy job hunters can reach OPM on the Internet at *fjob.opm.gov* for Telenet, or *ftp.fjob.opm.gov* for File Transfer Protocol. If all you have is e-mail, then send your request for information to *info@fjob.opm.gov* and wait for their reply.

If you are near a federal office building or an OPM office, stop in and use their Federal Job Information "Touch Screen" computer. You'll find plenty of information and you can even type in a request to have application packages and detailed information mailed to you.

FEDFAX is yet another way to get employment information from the OPM. You'll need a touch-tone telephone or fax machine. FEDFAX doesn't list vacancy announcements or job listings, but does let you request forms and other information to be faxed to you. They'll send your request to any fax machine on the planet, and you can reach them every day, 24 hours a day, at these numbers:

Atlanta	404-331-5267
Denver	303-969-7764
Detroit	313-226-2593
San Francisco	415-744-7002
Washington, D.C.	202-606-2600

Don't forget OPM's Web site at *www.usajobs.opm.gov* if you have access to the Internet. You'll find the full text of each job announcement, be able to read answers to FAQs (frequently asked questions), and have access to electronic and paper copies of application forms. You can complete some applications on-line and submit them electronically to save you even more time. This option is available for some job opportunities, but not all. Don't forget—the public library may have computers on hand for public use if you don't own one.

The Paper Mill

If you have a fear of paper cuts you might want to brace yourself. When you apply for jobs with the federal government you can expect loads of paperwork. It's crucial that you fill in all the appropriate blanks and turn in every piece of paper that's requested. Hiring announcements posted for federal job vacancies—for example, by the OPM or directly from a hiring agency—let you know exactly what you'll need to apply. For most federal jobs, you can apply using a resume, a form known as the Optional Application for Federal Employment (available through the OPM), or some similar kind of written statement.

You should know, too, that federal jobs are classified a certain way to indicate the experience, salary level, and other features of the job. These classifications are known as "grades." With your application, you usually need to write in the job title; the announcement number of the job; and the grade(s) assigned to the job.

Remember, whatever paperwork you submit must contain all the information that is requested in the job vacancy announcement and on the Optional Application form. At the same time, don't flood them with more information than they asked for! Keep your resume or application brief, yet complete. And, above all, make your work legible and neat. They can't process what they can't read.

Pack Your Bags

When you apply to, say, the Springfield Police Department in Missouri, you can be relatively sure which state you'll be calling home after you're hired. A job offer from the Feds, however, carries with it no such certainty. They'll be times in your career when you may be shuffled from one end of the country to the other to accommodate the needs of your department, although most agencies try to get you where you want to be. This can either mean "adventure" or "nightmare" to you, depending on how you feel about relocation. Before you seriously consider an application with a federal agency, you should decide how you feel about moving and discuss it with family members who might be affected by the change. As one official with the FBI commented:

> If you originally applied at the San Francisco field office you can bet
> that won't be where you'll go for your first assignment. We almost

never send you back to the field office where you first applied for your first assignment. There are exceptions, of course. . . .

Let's give you an idea of where some of your future partners live. As of June 1996, about half of all federal officers took assignments in:

- California (10,469)
- Texas (8,836)
- New York (6,556)
- the District of Columbia (6,508)
- Florida (4,980)
- New Hampshire (58) and Rhode Island (94)

Until you know if the federal level is for you, there's not much point in picking out a moving company. And you won't know if you are interested in a federal position until you have a good idea of what they do. So let's start with the Justice Department, the largest federal employer of armed agents.

THE U.S. DEPARTMENT OF JUSTICE

The Department of Justice, under the leadership of the U.S. Attorney General, employs thousands of lawyers, agents, and investigators. The department directs some of the most challenging law enforcement organizations in the federal government, including the INS, FBI, DEA, Bureau of Prisons, and the U.S. Marshals Service.

U.S. IMMIGRATION AND NATURALIZATION SERVICE (INS)

The INS is now home to the largest force of armed agents, surpassing the Bureau of Prisons and the FBI. From September 1993 to September 1996, the INS increased its agents from 3,965 to 5,878. National concerns over immigration led to this increase and the hiring is continuing.

The INS enforces and regulates federal laws regarding the immigration and naturalization of non-U.S. citizens. If you were to join this agency, your duties would include the apprehension and deportation of persons who are trying to enter this country illegally or who have already arrived illegally. You may also perform criminal investigations, port-of-entry inspection duties, and background investigations on persons applying for U.S. citizenship. You may be assigned as a Border Patrol Agent, an INS Special Agent, or an INS Immigration Inspector.

Border Patrol Agent

As a border patrol agent, you'd be one of many uniformed law enforcement agents assigned to guard the borders of the U.S.—roughly 8,000 miles of land and coastal territory. Your chief duty would be to detect and prevent the smuggling or entry of illegal aliens into the U.S.

Most of a border patrol agent's time is taken up with surveillance and search efforts. Your assignment could include combing mile after mile of rough, desolate territory using specially equipped pursuit vehicles: cars, jeeps, helicopters, aircraft, or patrol boats. To help out, ground points are set up with sensor equipment that sounds alarms at stationary duty posts when motion is detected. Of course nothing replaces good eyesight and standard-issue binoculars to watch for signs of illegal border activity!

Good detective skills will come in handy in this position because you'll be expected to detect signs of illegal entry: footprints, tire tracks, and slashed or broken fences. You'll also investigate leads, conduct routine inquiries to uncover smuggling operations, and check the citizenship and immigration status of farm and ranch workers. Border patrol agents also set up highway traffic stops and search public transportation sites and vehicles (buses, trucks, trains, airplanes and boats) to find illegal aliens.

Your other duties will include:

♦ assisting in the criminal prosecution or deportation of illegal aliens in your custody
♦ assisting in the criminal prosecution of suspects involved in smuggling illegal aliens
♦ assisting in court proceedings regarding petitions for citizenship

Qualifications

Applicants for border patrol agent positions must be U.S. citizens who are at least 18 but under 37 years of age at the time of appointment. You will need to pass a written civil service examination administered by the OPM, a personal interview, a physical exam (including vision and hearing tests), and a background investigation. Work experience is required, either paid or voluntary, although a full four-year course of college undergraduate study may be substituted for work experience.

One very important job requirement for active border patrol agents is the ability to read and speak Spanish at a highly-rated level (good to excellent). If you have this ability at the time you apply, you'll be given additional credit in the hiring process; otherwise, you will have to meet this requirement by the time you complete a one-year probationary period on the job. You shouldn't be surprised to hear that your first assignment will be in the southwest states bordering Mexico: California, Arizona, New Mexico, or Texas.

Training

Border patrol trainees participate in an 18-week training program at the Border Patrol Academy located at the Federal Law Enforcement Training Center in Glynco, Georgia. This training covers subject areas such as immigration and naturalization laws, criminal law, tracking methods, pursuit driving, arrest techniques, and firearms.

Applying for the Job

First, you'll need to find out when the appropriate civil service examination will be given by the OPM. You can contact the OPM office nearest to you or you can write to the Border Patrol's Special Examining Unit operated by the INS:

> The Immigration and Naturalization Service
> Border Patrol Examining Unit
> 425 I Street N.W., 2nd Floor
> Washington, D.C. 20536-0001

INS Special Agents

If border patrol agent is not exactly what you were looking for, you might find INS special agent more to your liking. Special agents are non-uniformed officers who plan and conduct investigations designed to uncover violations of criminal and statutory laws regulated by the INS. They gather information and evidence by reviewing public and private records and immigration documents, as well as by questioning informants and witnesses, and interrogating suspects.

As a special agent you may get the chance to set up complex surveillance and undercover operations. When your operation is successful and you catch your crooks in the act of a criminal violation, you'll have the pleasure of arresting the suspects and seizing the evidence. When the suspects are brought to trial, you'll be expected to assist in preparing the prosecution's case—that usually means a trip to the witness stand.

Qualifications

Applicants must be U.S. citizens between the ages of 21 and 37 at the time of appointment, although the upper age limitation may be waived if you now hold, or have held in the past, a federal law enforcement position. You will need to pass a personal interview, a physical exam (including vision and hearing tests), and a background investigation. Either a bachelor's degree, three years of work experience, or an equivalent combination of education and work experience are also required.

Training

New recruits face an 18-week training program at the Federal Law Enforcement Training Center in Glynco, Georgia. Coursework includes immigration and naturalization laws and investigative techniques, in addition to other relevant subjects.

Applying for the Job

To apply, you need to establish an eligibility rating with the OPM, either by taking a written test or completing a questionnaire describing your previous experience. Contact the INS for details at:

> The Immigration and Naturalization Service
> Border Patrol Examining Unit
> 425 I Street N.W., 2nd Floor
> Washington, D.C. 20536-0001

INS Immigration Inspectors

You aren't out of options with the INS yet. How about a career as an INS immigration inspector? Your job would be to allow the entry of eligible persons into the country, while preventing the entry of those who aren't allowed on U.S. soil. This is a uniformed position and you can expect to be stationed at either a land port, seaport, airport, and any other point of entry where travelers arrive from other countries. Immigration inspectors process literally millions of people each year from these locations, examining passports, visas, and other legal documentation. You'd be expected to keep up-to-date on the laws, regulations, policies, and court and administrative decisions that govern legal entry into the U.S.

Qualifications

To apply for this position, you must:

- be a U.S. citizen
- pass a personal interview

- pass a physical examination (including vision and hearing tests)
- pass a background investigation
- have either a bachelor's degree or at least three years of responsible work experience

There are *no* minimum or maximum age limits for becoming an INS immigration inspector.

Training

New hires participate in a 14-week training program at the Federal Law Enforcement Training Center in Glynco, Georgia. The program includes courses in Spanish, nationality laws, and firearms proficiency.

Applying for the Job

For information on testing and application procedures, you should contact either the OPM or the nearest INS regional office in:

- South Burlington, Vermont
- Dallas, Texas
- Fort Snelling, Minnesota
- Laguna Niguel, California

FEDERAL BUREAU OF INVESTIGATION (FBI)

The Mission of the FBI is to uphold the law through the investigation of violations of federal criminal law; to protect the United States from foreign intelligence and terrorist activities; to provide leadership and law enforcement assistance to federal, state, local, and international agencies; and to perform these responsibilities in a manner that is responsive to the needs of the public and is faithful to the Constitution of the United States.—FBI Mission Statement

This mission is exactly what makes the FBI a unique organization. You can be sure that the title "Special Agent" isn't given lightly. College graduates all across the nation compete heavily for the chance to work for the main investigative arm of the U.S. Department of Justice.

The FBI has responsibility for foreign counterintelligence matters, conducting background investigations on nominees for top jobs in the U.S.

government, and for criminal investigations that often cause headlines across the world (the World Trade Center bombing, for example). They have jurisdiction in more than 200 types of criminal cases, including bank robberies, espionage, terrorism, civil rights violations, fraud, and assassination attempts on federal officials.

Special Agent

Once you become a special agent, you'll work on high-security cases and have the FBI's sophisticated resources at your disposal; however, your basic duties will be the same as other law enforcement investigators. You'll hunt for facts and evidence that can be used to solve criminal cases; handle tons of paperwork; conduct undercover surveillance operations; question informants, witnesses, and suspects; and arrest suspects. At the end of it all, of course, you'll write detailed reports. The information and evidence you collect will be submitted to the appropriate U.S. Attorney or Department of Justice official for legal action, if warranted. If your case goes to trial, you'll testify in court when called.

The FBI divides its investigations into seven programs:

- Applicant Matters
- Civil Rights
- Counterterrorism
- Financial Crime
- Foreign Counterintelligence
- Organized Crime/Drugs
- Violent Crimes and Major Offenders

What makes the FBI different from many law enforcement agencies is their ability to devote intense investigative attention to individual cases, depending on the circumstances. Unlike police work, where investigators may be expected to work dozens of cases at the same time, special agents are often able to give their undivided attention to one case at a time.

The FBI does *not* go through the OPM when they hire for special agent positions—or for support personnel positions, for that matter. Because of the FBI's diverse responsibilities, they've been given more latitude in personnel matters than you'll see in most other federal agencies. Everyone who goes to work for the FBI is considered to be in the "excepted service"—that means FBI employees are *not* civil service employees. As a result, the Director of the FBI can make personnel decisions relating to hiring, applicant qualifications, promotions, and discipline that you wouldn't see if the agency operated under civil service regulations.

Qualifications

To be considered by the FBI, you must be a U.S. citizen between the ages of 23 and 37 upon appointment. You must have a bachelor's degree from an accredited four-year college or university and you must have three years of full-time work experience. If you are a law school graduate or a graduate in a field for which the FBI has a need, then they may waive the three-year work requirement.

The FBI will put you through your paces with a series of written tests that are computer-scored at FBI headquarters in Washington, D.C. After you make it over this hurdle, you'll participate in a formal interview, followed by an intense background investigation. Special agents in charge of your background investigation will be busy interviewing your neighbors, work associates, personal references, past employers, and family members, as well as verifying all the information you list on your application.

You'll be expected to pass a drug test and a polygraph examination. A physical examination may also be required. FBI personnel will go over the results of your background investigation and assess it for a final hiring decision.

The FBI has five entrance programs under which you may qualify to be hired as a special agent. These programs consider your education and work experience based on one of these five possibilities:

1. Law—graduates of an ABA-accredited law school who have two years of resident undergraduate work
2. Accounting—graduates of an accredited four-year college or university with a degree in accounting
3. Language—graduates of an accredited four-year college or university who are fluent in a foreign language for which the FBI has a current need
4. Diversified—graduates of an accredited four-year college or university who have at least three years of full-time work experience
5. Engineering/Science—graduates of an accredited college or university who have either a master's or other advanced degree in engineering or computer science; or a bachelor's degree in engineering or computer science and at least three years of work experience

Training

As a newly appointed special agent, you'll undergo 15 weeks of extensive training at the FBI Academy in Quantico, Virginia. Your classroom instruction includes a wide range of academic and investigative topics, as well as physical fitness, firearms training, and defensive tactics. Before graduation, you'll be trained in investigative, intelligence gathering, interview, and interrogation techniques.

Applying for the Job

To apply for a position with the FBI, you should contact the field office nearest to you. A list of those offices is in Appendix B. Be sure to check their Web site at *www.fbi.gov.*

DRUG ENFORCEMENT ADMINISTRATION (DEA)

The choices don't get any easier as we go along. And there's certainly nothing easy about getting into the DEA. This agency is deadly serious about their mission to enforce U.S. laws on illegal drug trafficking and their efforts to prevent drug abuse. To join the over 2,950 agents already there, you'll have to meet high qualifying standards, because the DEA's academic and physical training requirements are rugged. Mark these folks off your list if hard work doesn't appeal to you!

After hiring and training by the DEA, you will track down major suppliers of narcotics and other dangerous drugs in both the U.S. and abroad. Your focus will be on the distribution of illicit drugs such as heroin, cocaine, hallucinogens, and marijuana, as well as both illegal and legal trade in depressants, stimulants, and other controlled substances.

Special Agent

As a DEA special agent, your duties will be to uncover criminal drug activities and catch violators of federal drug laws so that they can be prosecuted. Because the DEA focuses primarily on large-scale illegal drug operations, you'll be taking on highly dangerous work. You'll be involved in planning and conducting investigations that target individuals and organizations who make and distribute illegal drugs and narcotics, and those who divert legal controlled substances for unlawful purposes. As you might expect, surveillance and undercover work will play a big role in this job.

DEA special agents collect information by following paper trails; questioning informants, witnesses, and suspects; and using top-notch investigative skills. After you've rounded up sufficient evidence and have plenty of probable cause, you'll arrest suspects and confiscate illegal drug supplies. Courts across the country will rely on the results of your investigation and your testimony to get convictions.

Some of your time may be spent passing on your knowledge of drug control and drug-related crime to other law enforcement professionals, communities, and organizations nationwide. You'll also be expected to work with other federal, state, and local law enforcement agencies. And you'll work with foreign governments, agencies, and law enforcement to help develop intelligence networks and investigate unlawful drug trade.

As you might expect, you must be willing to accept assignments anywhere in the United States upon appointment. The DEA will even have you sign a statement agreeing to this condition before giving you an offer of employment.

Qualifications

You must be a U.S. citizen between 21 and 36 years of age at the time of appointment, and you must possess a valid driver's license. You must also be in excellent physical condition, possess sharp hearing acuity, and have uncorrected vision of at least 20/200. If corrected, your vision can be 20/20 in one eye and 20/40 in the other. Unfortunately, the DEA disqualifies anyone who's had Radial Keratotomy (RK) surgery to correct vision problems.

The DEA asks that you have a college degree from an accredited college or university; it doesn't matter in what field of study. In addition, you'll need either one year of work experience or an overall GPA of 2.5 on a 4.0 scale and a GPA of 3.5 in your major field of study, with an academic standing in the upper 1/3 of a graduating class or major subdivision; membership in a scholastic honor society, and one year of graduate study.

You're not done yet! You must also make it through the special agent interview process, successfully complete a polygraph examination, psychological examination, and an intense background investigation. Your history of drug use, of course, will undergo close scrutiny. Drug screening is a part of the process, and once you are hired you will be subject to random testing throughout your career.

Training

All DEA special agent trainees participate in a 16-week DEA training program conducted at the FBI Academy in Quantico, Virginia. This course will include instruction on drug laws, drug identification, investigative techniques, arrest, search and seizure, ethics, self-defense, use of firearms, court procedures, and criminology. But before you earn your DEA badge, you'll be expected to pass this course of instruction, as well as a physical fitness test. New agents are required to complete a probationary/trial period of three to four years after successfully completing the basic training course.

Applying for the Job

More information is available about the DEA on their Web site at *www.usdoj.gov/dea.* Applications should be sent directly to the nearest DEA office for hiring consideration. You'll need to provide specific forms and documents with your application. This may include a resume or Optional Application for Federal Employment, a Background Survey Questionnaire (OPM Form 1386), and a college transcript. For specifics, call 1-800-DEA-4288 or write to:

> Drug Enforcement Administration
> Office of Personnel
> 1405 I Street N.W.
> Washington, D.C. 20537

BUREAU OF PRISONS

The Bureau of Prisons (BOP) is the second largest federal employer of sworn law enforcement personnel, employing more than 11,329 individuals. The BOP is responsible for hiring all corrections officers who work at federal prison institutions nationwide. Federal penal and correctional institutions are for people who have either violated or are awaiting trial for violating federal laws. This is where you will work if you pass muster with the BOP.

The need for federal corrections officers at new institutions, combined with a high turnover rate, makes the BOP one of the hot spots for federal employment opportunities. That doesn't mean it's easy, though! They have more competitive requirements for their corrections officers than most state or county correctional facilities. Having a bachelor's degree in psychology, criminology, or counseling will really get their attention because of BOP's emphasis on inmate rehabilitation.

Qualifications

As you've seen in the general description of duties outlined in chapter one of this book, corrections is a challenging field. To be hired by the BOP, you must have:

+ a four-year college degree, or
+ a minimum of three years of previous experience in law enforcement, corrections, or an area of general experience such as teaching, counseling, or parole/probation worker

Training

All federal corrections officers attend a 13-day, 120-hour training program at the federal training facility in Glynco, Georgia. Your transportation to Georgia and your room and board during training are paid for by the federal government. Training classes start at 7:30 a.m. and end at 4:30 p.m. Your classroom topics will include legal issues, communication, self-defense training, and firearms proficiency.

After the training program, you'll report for work at the facility that hired you. That facility will see to it that your training continues as you learn all about their policies and procedures. For one year you will be under probation and closely monitored by a supervisor.

Applying for the Job

To get into the selection process, you must fill out the OPM application form 1203AW Form C for the BOP. You can get this application by calling or writing to:

Federal Bureau of Prisons
National Recruitment Office
Room 460
Washington, DC 20534
202-307-1490

Information is also available on their Web site at *www.bop.gov*. Another way to get an application is to request one from the personnel office of any federal prison facility. You may also get an application by calling or writing to any regional BOP office. The regional BOP offices are located at:

Mid-Atlantic Regional Office	South Central Regional Office
10010 Junction Drive	4211 Cedar Springs Road, Suite 300
Suite 100-N	Dallas, TX 75219
Annapolis Junction, MD 20701	(214) 767-9700
(301) 317-3100	
	Southeast Regional Office
North Central Regional Office	523 McDonough Boulevard, S.E.
Gateway Complex Tower 11, 8th Floor	Atlanta, GA 30315
4th and State Avenue	(404) 624-5202
Kansas City, KS 66101	
(913) 621-3939	Western Regional Office
	7950 Dublin Boulevard, 3rd Floor
Northeast Regional Office	Dublin, CA 94568
U.S. Customs House, 7th Floor	(510) 803-4700
2nd and Chestnut Street	
Philadelphia, PA 19106	**Return Your Completed Applications to:**
(215) 597-6317	FBOP/Examining Section
	10010 Junction Drive, Suite 217 South
	Annapolis Junction, MD 20701

U.S. MARSHALS SERVICE

What most people think about when you bring up the U.S. Marshals Service is their famous Witness Protection Program, created in the 1970s. What you may not realize is this organization is the country's oldest federal law enforcement agency, having been established in 1789. It employs over 2,650 officers. Deputy U.S. marshals are hired to provide security in the federal courts as well as investigative and security services related to federal prisoners and fugitives. They also safeguard witnesses who testify against organized crime activities in federal and state court cases through the Witness Protection Program.

Deputy U.S. Marshal

Deputy U.S. marshals answer to U.S. marshals, who are appointed by the U.S. President to head the 94 judicial districts across the country. If you hire on with this agency, you'll be considered an officer of the federal court and you'll coordinate security operations during federal court cases; this means protecting federal judges, attorneys, and other court officials and participants. You'll also make sure that proper security systems and personnel are in place throughout federal court buildings. A deputy marshal's role is similar to that of a bailiff during state and local trials: maintaining order in the courtroom, restraining violent persons, conducting weapons searches, and serving as guards and escorts.

Deputy U.S. marshals also serve court orders, such as subpoenas or criminal warrants; seize and manage property from criminal activities; and maintain custody of federal prisoners. If you are assigned to the Witness Protection Program, you'll be responsible for the safety and well-being of federal witnesses against organized crime.

As a law enforcement agent of the Attorney General, U.S. Department of Justice, tracking federal fugitives will be one of your most important responsibilities. (A federal fugitive is someone who has either escaped from custody, violated patrol or probation guidelines, or failed to obey orders to appear in federal court.) The trail may take you through other states or outside U.S. borders. You may also be asked to help foreign countries by locating their fugitives who have escaped to the U.S.

If you set your sights high enough, you may become a member of a highly trained unit of the U.S. Marshals Service called the Special Operations Group (SOG). The SOG can be called out to help with national emergencies in any U.S. judicial district; members are on call 24 hours a day and can be assembled within hours to intervene in situations such as large-scale public riots or a crisis triggered by terrorism. The SOG is a voluntary unit, but membership is restricted to the most qualified, skilled, and physically fit. Members are chosen after they go through specialized training.

Qualifications

To qualify for a deputy U.S. marshal position, you must be a U.S. citizen between the ages of 21 and 37 at the time of appointment. You will need to pass a written test, which is administered by the OPM, as well as a personal interview, a physical exam (including vision, hearing and physical performance tests), and a background investigation. Minimum education/experience requirements can be satisfied with either a bachelor's degree from an accredited college or university; three years of responsible work experience; or an equivalent combination of education and work experience. (One academic year of full-time undergraduate study is considered equivalent to nine months of work experience.)

Training

You will be asked to complete a 13-week basic training program at the Federal Law Enforcement Training Center in Glynco, Georgia. This training consists of an eight-week criminal investigator's course and five weeks of courses related to the specific duties of a deputy U.S. marshal.

Applying for the Job

Test dates are subject to change, so your best bet is to contact the OPM or a U.S. marshals service field office. Testing information is available with a phone call to 202-307-9437. Check out their Web site at *www.usdoj.gov/Marshals* for additional information.

U.S. TREASURY DEPARTMENT

The U.S. Treasury Department's major duties include formulating economic, fiscal, and tax policies; enforcing federal laws; protecting the President and other officials; and overseeing the manufacturing of currency. The law enforcement arm of the U.S. Treasury Department includes a few well-known agencies you will want to investigate, namely the U.S. Customs Service, the U.S. Secret Service, and the ATF.

U.S. CUSTOMS SERVICE

If the INS isn't the employer for you, but you do find the idea of working America's ports of entry exciting, you'll probably find one of the oldest government agencies appealing: the U.S. Customs Service. This agency, established in 1789 by the first Congress of the United States, is duty-bound to regulate and enforce federal patent, trademark, and copyright laws, specifically by monitoring ports of entry into the country. All law enforcement officials employed by the U.S. Customs Services have duties that in one way or another support this overall mission. This includes efforts to prevent and intercept persons engaged in criminal acts such as illegal smuggling of merchandise and goods, revenue fraud on imported or exported goods, drug and arms trafficking, and cargo thefts.

Customs Special Agent

Your job as a customs special agent will resemble that of a police detective, although special agents operate under a much wider scope of authority and territory. The cases you will investigate fall under two related categories: stopping and prosecuting illegal imports and exports, and collecting revenue (tariff duties and taxes) owed to the government on legal imports and exports.

What you'll actually do on a day-to-day basis depends on the case to which you are assigned. If your case involves the collection of evidence and information, you may either investigate public and private records, or you may question suspects, witnesses, or other sources to get your information. Setting up complex surveillances and undercover operations will likely be in your future.

You won't be stuck inside an office as a special agent. Part of your job will be to search ships, aircrafts, and land vehicles. You'll seize smuggled goods and illegal shipments of narcotics, arms, and other contraband, as well as detain vehicles or vessels used to transport illegal or suspect goods. Of course, you'll have the authority to arrest persons connected with acts that violate federal laws governed by the U.S. Customs Service.

You'll have a wide range of cases to handle as a special agent: drug trafficking by organized crime syndicates, tax evasion by international businesses that falsify the value of otherwise legal shipments, and individuals failing to declare purchases made while visiting other countries. Whatever the case, an important part of your job will be to keep accurate records of your investigations so that criminal charges can be made and supported. And, as always, you will be a frequent visitor to the courtroom witness stand and an asset to the prosecutor who takes your case to trial.

Qualifications

To qualify for a customs agent position, you must be a U.S. citizen of at least 21 but under 37 years of age. You will need to take the Treasury Enforcement Agent (TEA) written examination, which is designed to gauge certain basic skills needed for investigative work, such as good judgment, logic, planning, and communication skills. You must pass the TEA, a physical examination (including vision and hearing tests), a background investigation, and a drug screening. In addition, you must have either a bachelor's degree from an accredited college in any field of study, or at least one year of general work experience and two years of related, specialized experience.

Training

Once accepted as a special agent recruit, you will participate in a 14-week enforcement training program at the Federal Law Enforcement Training Center in Glynco, Georgia. The program includes written tests, physical performance tests, and graded practical exercises. Areas covered by this training include the use of firearms, undercover and surveillance techniques, rules of evidence and courtroom procedures, customs laws and regulations, and various methods of investigation and law enforcement.

Applying for the Job

The TEA examination is administered by the OPM. More information on testing and application information is available from:

U.S. Customs Service
Office of Human Resources
Enforcement Division
P.O. Box 7108
Washington, D.C. 20044

Customs Inspector

As a customs inspector, you'll have a hands-on job tracking violations in federal customs and commerce laws. You'll be responsible for inspecting not only the personal baggage of travelers entering or leaving the U.S., but also large cargo transported by vehicles on land, air, and sea. In all cases, customs inspectors are trained to know what to look for and how to handle situations where laws have been violated. Your common sense, good observational powers, and instincts will serve you well in this position.

You won't be stuck inside an office with this job, either. In order for you to regulate commercial shipments, you'll be authorized to board and examine aircraft, ships, trains, and other vehicles of transport. Part of your job may be to examine cargo documentation as well as the actual cargo to ensure that no smuggling, fraud, or theft takes place. On a ship, for example, you may oversee the unloading of cargo containers, question crew and passengers, and conduct physical searches if any criminal activity is suspected. These efforts are aimed at uncovering the transport of illegal goods—such as narcotics or weaponry—plus goods that have been undervalued, have not been reported, or that exceed legal limits of the amount allowed in or out of the country.

The work of customs inspectors is to make sure duty fees are properly assessed and collected on items brought into the country. You have the authority to inspect baggage and search passengers to reveal whether undeclared goods are being carried or illegal goods are being smuggled. You can also detain and question passengers to determine whether intentional fraud was committed. If so, you'll seize items as evidence and report the incident for legal action by the U.S. Customs

Service. When the situation warrants, you are empowered to place individuals under arrest for later criminal prosecution.

Qualifications

In addition to being a U.S. citizen, you must pass a physical examination, a background investigation, and a drug test. You will need to have either a bachelor's degree from an accredited college or at least three years of responsible work experience. A written test—the Customs Inspector Examination—is also administered to applicants for this position. However, by meeting certain educational standards you may be eligible for an Outstanding Scholar Program. Specifically, you must have graduated from college with either a GPA of at least 3.4 on a 4.0 scale; or been in the upper 10% of your graduating class. If you meet either of these standards, the written test may be waived.

Training

As a customs inspector recruit, you will participate in an 11-week enforcement training program at the Federal Law Enforcement Training Center in Glynco, Georgia. This training includes a series of written and physical tests as well as graded practical exercises (firearms proficiency, for example).

Applying for the Job

The Customs Inspector Examination is administered by the Customs Service. More information on testing and application procedures is available through:

> U.S. Customs Service
> Office of Human Resources
> Operations Division
> P.O. Box 14156
> Washington, D.C. 20044

Three other law enforcement positions are available through the U.S. Customs Service to serve the overall goals of this agency: canine enforcement officer; customs pilot; and import specialist. They each have duties that bring them together regularly with special agents and customs inspectors to investigate customs-related violations. The job qualifications differ in some significant ways, however. These positions are highly specialized and require certain technical expertise or an aptitude in particular areas.

Customs Canine Enforcement Officers

This job will capture the heart of the dog-loving law enforcement professional. Customs canine enforcement officers are responsible for training and handling dogs to uncover the smuggling of illegal narcotics and dangerous drugs, including marijuana, cocaine, heroin, and other controlled substances. If you are chosen for this position, you'll be assigned to ports of entry across the U.S., and will play a vital role in searching suspect persons and property. Canine enforcement officers are often called in to assist with formal investigations, such as those conducted by customs special agents, leading to the apprehension and arrest of smugglers.

Qualifications

To qualify for this position you must be a U.S. citizen; pass a physical examination, background investigation, and drug screening; and have at least three years of responsible work experience or a bachelor's degree from an accredited college. You will not need to take a written test. Related experience, especially any that demonstrates an affinity for dogs, is an obvious plus.

Once selected as a recruit, you will participate in 10 weeks of enforcement and dog handler training at the U.S. Customs Service Canine Enforcement Training Center in Front Royal, Virginia. This training includes written and physical tests as well as graded practical exercises, including one on firearms proficiency.

Applying for the Job

Recruitment bulletins are issued by the OPM when the U.S. Customs Service has openings for this position. More information on testing and application procedures is available through:

U.S. Customs Service
Office of Human Resources
Operations Division
P.O. Box 14060
Washington, D.C. 20044

Customs Pilot

Customs pilots are licensed, experienced pilots who conduct air surveillance to detect customs violations using a specially equipped fleet of planes and helicopters (which are maintained by the Customs Service). If flying is your first love, you might be well-suited to this job. Flight duties could involve identifying illegal traffic on the U.S. borders between Mexico and Canada, or pursuing smugglers by air along coastal areas. Not boring work, by any stretch of the imagination! Customs pilots are also authorized to detain and question suspects, conduct physical searches, and make arrests.

Qualifications

This position has strict technical requirements, which include holding a current Federal Aviation Agency (FAA) commercial pilot's license and passing a current FAA Class I physical examination. In addition, you must be a U.S. citizen of at least 21 but under 37 years of age, and pass a background investigation and a drug screening. The U.S. Customs Service will determine your eligibility based on your application and your Record of Aeronautical Experience (Form OPM-1170-21).

Training

Those selected as recruits will participate in a 16-week enforcement training program at the Federal Law Enforcement Training Center in Glynco, Georgia. This training includes written and physical tests as well as graded practical exercises, including one on firearms proficiency.

Applying for the Job

More information on testing and application procedures is available through:

> U.S. Customs Service
> Office of Human Resources
> Delegated Examining Unit/Pilots
> P.O. Box 14060
> Washington, D.C. 20044

Customs Import Specialists

Customs import specialists perform a variety of administrative and investigative functions, primarily related to revenue collection on imported goods. The word "specialist" in this title indicates skill in appraising the value of commercial imports and calculating payments owed the government on such shipments. If you are hired in this capacity, you'll work with other customs officials and you may request to assist in formal investigations into illegally suspect shipments, incidents of fraud, and schemes aimed at dodging tariff and trade laws.

Qualifications

Requirements for this position include being a U.S. citizen of at least 21 but under 37 years of age and passing a physical examination, a background investigation, and a drug screening. You also must have at least three years of progressively responsible work experience or equivalent education (one academic year of full-time undergraduate study equals nine months of work experience). To help gauge your own interest in this position, keep in mind that enforcing the law in this case means having an aptitude for math, economics, paperwork, and understanding complex trade regulations.

A written test is required before you can take on this position. The ACWA (Administrative Careers With America) Examination for Law Enforcement and Investigative Positions is administered by the OPM. You will need to submit an Admission Notice and Record Card (Form 5000-B) to the OPM location where you want to take the test. The OPM will return the admission notice to you to tell you when and where to report for the test.

Training

Once accepted as a recruit, you will participate in six weeks of technical training at the Federal Law Enforcement Training Center in Glynco, Georgia. This training includes a series of written and graded practical exercises.

Applying for the Job

More information on testing and application procedures is available through:

U.S. Customs Service
Office of Human Resources
Operations Division
P.O. Box 14156
Washington, D.C. 20044

U.S. SECRET SERVICE

There probably isn't a soul in the U.S. who isn't aware of the most visible responsibility of this organization: the protection of the U.S. President, Vice President, their families, and other government officials. Special agents of the Secret Service handle security operations when these officials are traveling. Officers in a special unit—the U.S. Secret Service Uniformed division—provide security at the White House, at the official residence of the Vice President, and foreign diplomatic missions (primarily in the Washington, D.C. area).

When the Secret Service was founded in 1865, its mission was to investigate the counterfeiting of U.S. currency, and to uncover other forms of currency fraud. The U.S. Secret Service has over 3,000 agents assigned to its different divisions. Here's a look at some of the titles you could someday carry.

Special Agent

Special agents are charged with the duty of protecting:

- the President, Vice President, President-elect, Vice President-elect, and their immediate families
- former Presidents, their spouses or widows (until remarriage), and their minor children
- major Presidential and Vice Presidential candidates within 120 days of a general presidential election
- visiting heads of foreign states or governments

As a special agent, you may also be assigned by the President to guard other foreign dignitaries visiting the U.S., or official representatives of the U.S. while they are on missions abroad.

A significant part of your protective duties will be making sure that all necessary security measures are in place for public appearances. An advance team of special agents will scope out locations to determine methods of transportation, travel routes, the type of personnel and security equipment needed, and alternate routes and facilities to be used in case of an emergency. You'll be expected to make use of highly sophisticated communications and surveillance equipment to carry out your assignments. Special agents also rely upon other federal, state, and local law enforcement agencies for a helping hand with anything from background information to equipment and personnel.

As important as the protective duties are, there's yet another serious area of responsibility, and that's the investigation of currency fraud. This includes counterfeiting operations; the forgery or theft of U.S. Government checks, bonds, and securities; and credit card, computer, and electronic transfer fraud. If you are assigned to a fraud case, you'll gather background data and evidence; arrange for surveillance and/or undercover work; question informants, witnesses, and suspects; arrest suspects; and seize evidence. When the bad guys are brought to trial, your reports will help the U.S. Attorneys, as will your testimony in court.

Qualifications

Before you can be hired as a special agent you must be a U.S. citizen of at least 21 but under 37 years of age at the time of appointment, and you must pass the following:

- a written exam (the TEA Examination)
- a personal interview
- a polygraph exam
- a background investigation
- a medical exam (including vision and hearing tests)

A bachelor's degree from an accredited college or university in any field of study is also required. You may be able to qualify instead with at least three years of work experience, two of those in criminal investigative work; or with the equivalent in relevant work experience and education.

Don't forget. . . you must be willing to travel and to relocate at any time!

Training

As a special agent recruit, you'll receive general investigative training at the Federal Law Enforcement Training Center in Glynco, Georgia. You'll also receive specialized instruction at the Secret Service training facilities near Washington, D.C. This course of training includes protective techniques, criminal law, the use of firearms, defensive measures, surveillance techniques, and undercover operations.

Applying for the Job

To apply and sign up to take the Treasury Enforcement Agent (TEA) Examination, contact the nearest OPM or Secret Service field office. Information is available on their Web site at *www.treas.gov/USSS*. To get the most up-to-date information, dial 1-800-827-7783, or write:

U.S. Secret Service Personnel Division
1800 G Street, N.W.
Washington, D.C. 20223

Uniformed Division Officer

You'll be a bit more visible in the capacity of uniformed division officer. You'll be asked to perform high-level security and law enforcement functions as a member of this division and you'll be assigned to the Washington, D.C. metropolitan area to cover security for:

- the White House grounds and any buildings which house presidential offices
- the official residence of the Vice President
- foreign diplomatic missions or embassies located in the District of Columbia (or other regions under special order of the President)

The uniformed division operates much like a police force, constantly on the watch for any disturbances, suspicious situations, and criminal activity. As an officer, your job will be to make sure all the necessary security systems and equipment are in place. You'll also conduct regular patrols to monitor the grounds, buildings, and security equipment in your assigned area. Officers are assigned to fixed security posts at entrance and exit points to ensure that visitors are authorized to be on the premises. You'll have the authority to question, search, and arrest trespassers or others involved in illegal or disruptive activities.

Qualifications

To qualify for the uniformed division, you must be a U.S. citizen of at least 21 but under 37 years of age at the time of appointment. Once you have passed a written exam, you'll go through a personal interview. You must also pass a background investigation, a polygraph test, and a medical examination (including vision and hearing tests.) A high school diploma or GED satisfies the minimum educational requirements.

Training

Uniformed division officer recruits are trained at the Federal Law Enforcement Training Center in Glynco, Georgia and receive specialized instruction at the Secret Service training facilities near Washington, D.C. This training includes courses in police procedures; psychology; police-community relations; criminal law; first aid; laws of arrest; search and seizure; use of firearms; and defensive tactics.

Applying for the Job

Tests and interviews are conducted by the U.S. Secret Service. The written exam is usually given on a quarterly basis in the Washington, D.C. area and periodically in other major U.S. cities. To apply to take the test, you need to submit a 3x5 index card or postcard stating your name, address, and telephone numbers (home and work). On this card you'll also need to indicate where you want to be tested: in Washington, D.C., in a major city in your area, or in any city where the test is given. Send your card to:

U.S. Secret Service
Attn: Uniformed Division Recruiter
1800 G Street, N.W.
Washington, D.C. 20223

For further information, call the Secret Service at 1-800-827-7783.

BUREAU OF ALCOHOL, TOBACCO, AND FIREARMS (ATF)

The ATF is another possible home for those who dislike boredom. Over 1,900 ATF officers enforce federal laws and regulations controlling alcohol, tobacco, firearms, explosives, and arson. The mission for these men and women is to:

♦ reduce violent crime
♦ protect the public
♦ collect revenue from legal trade within certain industries

The ATF strives to prevent the illegal possession, use, and trafficking of liquor, cigarettes and guns. Many bombing incidents and for-profit arson schemes also fall under the ATF's jurisdiction.

Special Agent

Like most federal agencies, the ATF works closely with other federal, state, and local law enforcement agencies. Depending on the case on which you are working, you may set up surveillance operations, work undercover, or participate in a raid. Your duties as a special agent will also include investigating arson and bombing incidents and the trafficking of ammunition and bombing devices, which frequently involve organized crime or terrorist groups. You'll be authorized to conduct legal searches and seize contraband and physical evidence. After the arrests are made and the reports written, you'll help prepare cases for criminal prosecution and give court testimony when called to the witness stand.

Qualifications

Among the requirements for on ATF special agent position, you must be a U.S. citizen of at least 21 but under 37 years of age at the time of appointment. A four-year degree from an accredited college or university is required. In some cases, the equivalent in work experience, or education plus work experience, may be considered instead.

Your vision has to be within acceptable levels: distance vision without correction must be at least 20/100 in each eye, correctable to 20/30 in one eye and 20/20 in the other. You must pass an exhaustive background investigation, a medical examination, and a drug screening; your weight must be in good proportion to your height.

The Treasury Enforcement Agent (TEA) Exam

Before you get too far in the process you will need to take the Treasury Enforcement Agent (TEA) written examination. You can take this test at the nearest OPM office only when the ATF gives permission for it to be given on their behalf. After you pass this exam, your name is added to a roster of eligible candidates ranked by test score results. The names of the top four or five candidates are sent to the ATF by the OPM. The ATF takes it from there.

You may contact your local OPM area office regarding the TEA examination. Remember, they cannot offer the TEA exam unless the ATF requests it. Also, if you have taken the TEA exam through the Secret Service, you should be aware that the ATF will *not* accept that exam score because the Secret Service administers this test without competition. Special agent positions with the ATF are considered competitive.

Training

As a special agent trainee, you'll receive eight weeks of training in general law enforcement and investigative techniques at the Federal Law Enforcement Training Center in Glynco, Georgia. This training includes courses in surveillance techniques, rules of evidence, undercover assignments, arrest and raid techniques, and the use of firearms. Later, you'll receive "new agent training," covering the specific duties of ATF special agents such as instruction related to laws enforced by the ATF Bureau, case report writing, firearms and explosives operations, bomb scene searches, and arson investigations.

Applying for the Job

ATF does not keep a list of qualified applicants. If you want to be considered for a position with them you will have to watch for a specific vacancy announcement number. ATF posts current vacancy announcements through the OPM. When you see the announcement number you want, get a copy of the announcement and contact the OPM for the proper paperwork. All of the announcements will have a job description, qualifications for the job, deadlines for application submission, and application procedures. Check the beginning of this chapter for instructions on getting what you need from the OPM. You can also call the ATF's hotline at 202-927-8423, (TDD: 202-927-7941). Information is also available at *www.atf.treas.gov.*

THE U.S. GENERAL SERVICES ADMINISTRATION (GSA)

The General Services Administration is one of the three central management agencies in the federal government. Its mission is to provide space, supplies, services, and work environments. You'll find representatives of the GSA wherever federal employees are at work.

FEDERAL PROTECTIVE SERVICE

The Federal Protective Service (FPS) is the security branch of the U.S. General Services Administration (GSA), a huge government agency that performs numerous managerial functions related to civilian work sites owned or leased by the federal government. One of the GSA's most important functions—that of ensuring the protection of life and property at these work sites nationwide—is carried out by the Federal Protective Service.

The FPS maintains a mobile, uniformed police force of over 600 professionals known as federal protective officers. They enforce laws, provide security services, and perform general policing duties on GSA-controlled federal properties. The FPS also maintains a force of nonuniformed criminal investigators who investigate crimes committed on these properties, often working with local and other law enforcement agencies.

Federal Protective Officer

As a federal protective officer, your main responsibilities will be to establish proper security measures and preserve law and order. You can expect assignment to civilian work sites that are owned or leased by the federal government, where you will protect the employees of and visitors to these work sites as well as the actual physical property, buildings, and grounds.

Patrol duties include checking for signs of intrusion, damage, tampering, or unsafe conditions at the facilities in your charge. One of your duty assignments may be to watch over entrances to these areas to make sure that only federal employees and authorized visitors are admitted. Or, you may monitor electronic security systems which range from fire alarms to surveillance devices designed to detect intruders, criminal activity, or safety hazards.

When you wear the uniform of a federal protective officer, your role will be to keep the peace and prevent or suppress unlawful conduct. You will have the authority to question suspects, issue citations, make arrests, and seize evidence relative to crimes committed on the federal property to which you are assigned. These crimes could include burglary, physical assault, arson, disturbing the peace, instigating a riot, or unlawful assembly. You will handle emergency situations such as fires, bomb threats, and natural disasters.

Qualifications

To qualify for this position, you must be a U.S. citizen of at least 21 years of age. You'll need to pass a written test, a personal interview, a physical examination (including vision and hearing tests), a drug screening, and a background investigation. Other requirements include at least one year of police experience, or an equivalent amount of college education as determined by the Federal Protective Service.

Training

Trainees participate in an eight-week police training course at the Federal Law Enforcement Training Center in Glynco, Georgia. Specialized training is also provided in crowd and riot control techniques and in performing police functions that have an impact on national security.

Applying for the Job

The written test is administered by the OPM. If you pass this test, you will be put on an eligibility list for federal protective officer positions. More information on testing and application procedures is available through the nearest FPS office or by calling 202-501-0887. You can also contact:

Federal Protective Service
Room 2306
18th and F Streets N.W.
Washington, D.C. 20405

THE INSIDE TRACK

Who:	Jeremy J. Farner
What:	Border Patrol Agent
Where:	California in the San Diego Sector, Chula Vista Station
How long:	Over two years

Insider's Advice

I got involved with law enforcement when I was 14 through the Port Orange, FL, Police Explorer Program under Sergeant Neil Cascone—a great police officer and youth leader. The idea of being able to help people and make a difference was what made me go into this field. I also work for the National Crime Prevention Council as a crime prevention instructor, a team building instructor, and a gang instructor; I also work as a sector recruiter and explorer advisor for the Boy Scouts of America.

Insider's Take on the Future

If you want to work for the Border Patrol or in other law enforcement agencies, you should work on your skills and your grammar (English and Spanish), and be in decent shape. The job can be very physical, depending on the area of assignment.

I am proud of my profession and what I do. I try to bring as much professionalism to it as possible.

CHAPTER | 3

This chapter is designed to help you make crucial education and training decisions before you start knocking on employers' doors. You'll learn how the right education can put money in your pocket once you're employed, along with which colleges and universities offer the programs you'll need to succeed. Comments and advice from future employers and from educators complete the chapter.

LAW ENFORCEMENT EDUCATION AND TRAINING

Law enforcement has gotten *so* competitive over the past few years that most agencies will ask to see a transcript showing some college hours, if not an associate (two-year) degree or a bachelor's (four-year) degree before they'll consider you. The FBI, for example, won't even process your application without proof of your success at an accredited four-year college or university.

Frank Marousek, Assistant Dean of Admissions for John Jay College, thinks law enforcement and higher education are joining forces across the U.S.:

> I think the days of graduating high school or getting a GED and then going right into law enforcement are just about gone. Many police agencies in the nation require college credit or a degree as a prerequisite for appointment.

You don't need clues to figure out why this makes sense. When law enforcement employers hang out their "help wanted" sign, it's a sure bet that they'll focus on the most highly qualified and capable candidates. They'll prefer recruits who not only can get quickly up to speed on complex issues like deadly force and the laws of the land, but who can also add a healthy dose of common sense and good judgment to their list of talents. Since the competition is stiff, recruiters will be looking for solid evidence that you are exactly what they want.

THE COLLEGE DEBATE

Not everyone plans to or even wants to attend college. It takes time, money, dedication, and self-discipline to earn a degree. But let's be realistic. Put yourself in the shoes of a recruiting officer. You've got a pile of applications on your desk and some of them are from people who attended college. A recruiter can assume several things about these college-educated applicants: they made a commitment, and they were responsible enough to show up for classes and to study hard enough to pass their finals. They listened to lectures, participated in class discussions and projects, read books, wrote papers, took tests—all of which improved their communication and problem-solving skills. So, when it comes time to hire people who are likely to make it through page after page of state, local, or federal laws; write coherent, informative reports; and communicate well with a variety of people, you shouldn't be surprised when agencies lean toward candidates with proven track records.

However, a college degree isn't the only way you can show a future employer that you have similar qualities. Your life experiences, work background, and/or military training say a lot about you and will be considered heavily. But law enforcement recruiters also know that applicants who've had college experience are going to be better equipped to handle growth and change as law enforcement becomes more and more sophisticated in its strategies, methods, and technologies. Even your future co-workers are pushing for better-educated law enforcement professionals. A group of officers across the nation recently formed a non-profit organization known as the American Police Association, a professional organization for college-educated officers. If you'd like more information, you can reach them at this address:

American Police Association
5200 Leeward Lane, Suite 102
Alexandria, VA 22315
(703) 971-7935
FAX: (703) 922-2768
E-Mail: Apai@Wizard.net

EDUCATION PAYS OFF—LITERALLY

If you aren't yet convinced that getting more education is in your best interest, you might be pleased to find out that many law enforcement agencies, especially police departments, are willing to pay you extra for those college hours and/or degrees. Many police employers will add a bonus to starting base salaries, usually *after* you successfully complete academy training. The chart below gives a few examples of how education can pay off. The numbers in the "Bonus Pay Added to Base" column is how much extra they add to your base salary in return for the number of college hours you earned or the kind of degree you have.

Department	College hours or degree	Bonus Pay Added to Base
Orlando Police Dept. (FL)	2-year	$360 per year
	4-year	$960 per year
Atlanta Police Dept. (GA)	2-year	$1,622 per year
	4-year	$2,886 per year
Dallas Police Dept. (TX)	90 hrs	$720 per year
	4-year	$1,200 per year
Fort Worth Police Dept. (TX)	2-year	$720 per year
	4-year	$1,440 per year
Houston Police Dept. (TX)	60 hrs	$664.80 per year
	120 hrs	$1,329.84 per year
	4-yr + 6 yrs of service	$1,656 per year
Metropolitan Police Department of Nashville and Davidson County (TN)	2-year 4-year	$765.96 per year $1,531.80 per year
San Antonio Police Dept. (TX)	2-year	$1,800 per year
	4-year	$3,000 per year

Many departments offer a tuition reimbursement program as well, so once you are hired, if you start college (or go back to finish your degree), you'll receive financial assistance. You aren't going to get a totally free ride, of course. These departments usually want to see proof of passing grades before they chip in on the bill. And, yes, in some cases how much they chip in will depend on what grade you earn. The San Antonio Police Department, for example, pays 100% of your tuition if you make an "A," 75% for a "B," and 50% for a "C." Some departments will only pay for classes related to your job. "Job-related" may be defined in a detailed formal policy, or you may have to get your classes approved on a case-by-case basis.

Some departments make it even easier to attend college by permitting supervisors to adjust your work shifts and schedules so that you can attend classes. Other agencies offer scholarships or other financial incentives not only for college classes, but also for advanced state certification courses and certain in-service training programs. However and whenever you can manage it, your best chance to stay competitive for the best jobs and promotions in law enforcement is to get a quality education. Dean Marousek agrees:

> It bodes well for anyone to go to college first, or go to college while they are working or while they are in the military. You are going to need it eventually. Here in the New York City Police Department, if you want to be promoted you have to have at least 60 credits. The level of education you need increases as you go up the ranks.

Employers aren't going to hold it against you if you have a degree in a field other than criminal justice. Let's face it, most law enforcement agencies smile on candidates who have a college education in *any* field of study. It's hard to name a field that wouldn't be useful to law enforcement in some capacity: business, psychology, foreign languages, computer science, communications, English, public administration—all can be applied to law enforcement in some way. Beyond the book learning, there's the priceless value of being exposed to new ways of thinking and to people from different walks of life.

How to Choose the Right Program

It certainly helps to know what degree program to choose if you are aware of which law enforcement career you want. If policing is what you want to do, or you just aren't sure what kind of law enforcement you prefer, studying criminal justice or law enforcement administration/policing can be a good place to start. In the 1960s and 1970s, the FBI didn't want your application unless you were a CPA, a lawyer, or accountant. According to a top official, the FBI decided they didn't want to limit their applicant pool, so they began asking for men and women with different academic and professional backgrounds. Don't be shy about asking people who are already in the field that interests you how they got there. Ask them about their education: how they liked it, how valuable it's proven to be, and what they'd do differently if they could attend college all over again.

As you'll see by the extensive list provided at the end of this section, hundreds of colleges and universities offer what you'll need. Take the time to contact counselors and advisors about their programs. Ask *lots* of questions! Best advice of all—go for the *quality* of the education first in any field of study.

Be sure to ask about internships in criminal justice, law enforcement, and corrections programs. As many experts will tell you, internships—both paid and unpaid—are excellent ways to get your foot in the door. If you're specifically thinking about taking some law enforcement-related courses, check whether there are any colleges and police departments in your area working together. Many colleges hire police officers to teach criminal justice courses, and these are exactly the kinds of contacts that can prove invaluable. You might get ahead of the game not only with the classes you take, but with the network of contacts you make within them.

Going After the College Experience

Let's assume we've made our case and your thoughts are turning to higher education. What's your first step? Well, it's not what you might expect. Finding the money to go to school should *not* be your first concern, according to college and university admissions counselors. Your job is to choose the college or university that you think will best suit your needs, likes, and goals.

Most people aren't very good at doing something they genuinely hate—that's human nature. If you can't stand the thought of going to a huge school in a sprawling metropolis, then don't even consider it! There are over 500 two-year colleges and over 560 four-year colleges and universities in the U.S. that offer courses in criminal justice, and most of them aren't so big that you have to pack a lunch for the trip from one class to the next. Your environment needs to be a source of comfort and support, not an obstacle.

Another part of the college environment to consider is the student body composition. Would you feel more comfortable in an all-male or all-female environment, or do you prefer a co-ed setting? Granted, going to college is serious business, but it doesn't mean that you must cut yourself off from all human contact! Part of the value of a college education is learning to interact with people from all kinds of backgrounds and with many different experiences. You can get that experience in all three settings, so choose the one with which you are the most comfortable.

And how about class size? If you see a class so large it would take the professor 45 minutes to conduct a roll call, and you think you'd prefer a more personalized approach to learning, then you should consider enrolling in a medium- to small-sized college or university. Before you start packing your bags, ask yourself the following questions:

- Why am I going to college?
- Should I go "away" to college or stay in my home town?
- Do I want to live on-campus or off-campus?
- Do I want to attend a small college or huge university?
- Do I want to commit to a two-year or four-year program?

Once you have the answers, you'll be moving in the right direction.

There's no substitute for the advice of an experienced high-school guidance counselor or career counselor, so don't be shy about contacting one. Keep asking questions—of yourself and them—until you have the information you need to make your decision. And don't forget to chat with people who've "been there and done that." If you have a college in mind, but don't know anyone who's taken classes there, call the admissions department and see if they can put you in touch with students or alumni who'll be willing to talk about their experiences—the good and bad!

They're Not All the Same

There's more than one kind of institution of higher education, and it can become confusing when you're trying to figure out which one best suits your needs. Here are a few very basic definitions that might give you a better idea of what's available.

Community Colleges

These are public institutions offering vocational and academic courses. You need a high school diploma or GED to get in. Community colleges commonly offer a number of courses at night, making it easier on those who work daytime hours. It doesn't cost as much to attend a community college as it does a private institution or a public four-year college or university. Most programs require two years, or less, to complete. Depending on your course of study at a community college, you could have one of the following when you are finished:

- a certificate
- a license
- an AA degree (associate of arts)
- an AS degree (associate of science)
- an AAS degree (associate of applied science)

Junior Colleges

Junior colleges are (usually) privately owned two-year institutions. They tend to be more expensive than community colleges because they are privately owned. You can earn a two-year degree (AA or AS), which can usually be applied to four-year programs at most colleges and universities.

Colleges and Universities

Undergraduate programs (usually four-year) courses and graduate-level courses are offered at these institutions. Here you can earn a bachelor's degree in a variety of fields. Entrance requirements are more stringent than for community colleges; admissions personnel will expect you to have taken certain classes in high school to meet their admission standards. Some institutions ask that your high school GPA (grade point average) be above a certain level before they'll grant you admission. If your high school grades are weak or it's been some time since you were last in school, you might want to consider taking courses at a community college to bring you up to speed. You can always apply to the college or university as a transfer student after your academic track record has improved. Graduate degrees are available at most of these institutions if you choose to pursue one.

One piece of information to consider: public colleges and universities are less expensive to attend than private colleges and universities because they receive state funds to offset their operational costs.

DIRECTORY OF CRIMINAL JUSTICE TRAINING PROGRAMS

To aid your research, we've developed a list of institutions that offer degrees in criminal justice, law enforcement/policing, and corrections. Be aware that schools add and delete programs from their curriculum, so check for changes with the individual school.

If the school you are interested in offers ROTC programs, you will see the programs listed at the end of the school's profile.

Alabama

Alabama State University
915 S. Jackson St.
Montgomery, AL 36101-0271
(334) 229-4100
Criminal Justice
Air Force ROTC

Athens State College
300 N. Beaty St.
Athens, AL 35611
(205) 233-8100
Criminal Justice

Auburn University at Montgomery
7300 University Dr.
Montgomery, AL 36117-3596
(334) 244-3000
Criminal Justice
Army ROTC
Air Force ROTC

Jacksonville State University
N. Pelham Rd.
Jacksonville, AL 36265
(205) 782-5781
Criminal Justice
Army ROTC

Northwest Shoals Community
College
P.O. Box 2545
Muscle Shoals, AL 35662
(205) 331-5200
Criminal Justice

The University of Alabama
P.O. Box 870166
Tuscaloosa, AL 35487-0166
(205) 348-6010
Criminal Justice
Army ROTC
Air Force ROTC

Troy State University at Dothan
3601 U.S. 231 N
Dothan, AL 36303
(334) 983-6556
Criminal Justice

Troy State University at Main Campus
University Ave.
Troy, AL 36082
(205) 670-3000
Criminal Justice
Corrections
Air Force ROTC

Arizona

Arizona State University at Main
Campus
Tempe, AZ 85287
(602) 965-9011
Criminal Justice
Army ROTC
Air Force ROTC

Arizona Western College
P.O. Box 929
Yuma, AZ 85366
(520) 726-1000
Criminal Justice
Law

Grand Canyon University
3300 W Camelback Rd.
Phoenix, AZ 85017
(602) 249-3300
Criminal Justice
Army ROTC
Air Force ROTC

Ottawa University at Phoenix
2340 W Mission Ln.
Phoenix, AZ 85021
(602) 371-1188
Criminal Justice

Pima Community College
2202 W Anklam Rd.
Tucson, AZ 85709-0001
(520) 748-4500
Criminal Justice
Corrections
Army ROTC
Navy ROTC
Air Force ROTC

Arkansas

Northwest Arkansas Community
College
One College Dr.
Bentonville, AR 72712
(501) 619-4109
Criminal Justice

University of Arkansas at
Fayetteville
Administration Bldg. 422
Fayetteville, AR 72701
(501) 575-2000
Criminal Justice
Army ROTC
Air Force ROTC

University of Arkansas at Little
Rock
2801 S University Ave.
Little Rock, AR 72204
(501) 569-3000
Criminal Justice
Law
Army ROTC

University of Arkansas at Pine Bluff
1200 N University Box 4921
Pine Bluff, AR 71611
(501) 543-8000
Criminal Justice
Army ROTC

California

California Lutheran University
60 W Olsen Road
Thousand Oaks, CA 91360-2787
(805) 492-2411
Criminal Justice

Chapman University
333 N Glassell
Orange, CA 92866
(714) 997-6815
Criminal Justice
Army ROTC
Air Force ROTC

Pasadena City College
1570 E Colorado Blvd.
Pasadena, CA 91106
(818) 585-7123
Criminal Justice

Pitzer College
1050 N Mills Ave.
Claremont, CA 91711-6110
(909) 621-8198
Criminal Justice

Sacramento City College
3835 Freeport Blvd.
Sacramento, CA 95822
(916) 558-2111
Criminal Justice

Southwestern College
900 Otay Lakes Rd.
Chula Vista, CA 91910
(619) 421-67
Criminal Justice
Corrections
Law

Colorado

Regis University
3333 Regis Blvd.
Denver, CO 80221-1099
(303) 458-4100
Criminal Justice
Corrections

Connecticut

437 Pequot Ave.
New London, CT 06320
(860) 701-5000
Criminal Justice

Sacred Heart University
5151 Park Ave.
Fairfield, CT 06432-1023
(203) 371-7999
Criminal Justice
Army ROTC

University of New Haven
300 Orange Ave.
West Haven, CT 06516
(203) 932-7000
Criminal Justice
Law

Delaware
Delaware State University
1200 N Dupont Hwy.
Dover, DE 19901
(302) 739-4000
Criminal Justice
Army ROTC
Air Force ROTC

District of Columbia
American University
4400 Massachusetts Ave. NW
Washington, DC 20016
(202) 885-1000
Criminal Justice
Army ROTC
Navy ROTC
Air Force ROTC

George Washington University
2121 Eye St. NW
Washington, DC 20052
(202) 994-1000
Criminal Justice
Navy ROTC

Florida
Barry University
11300 N E 2nd Ave.
Miami, FL 33161
(305) 899-3000
Criminal Justice
Army ROTC
Air Force ROTC

Florida Agricultural and
Mechanical University
Tallahassee, FL 32307
(904) 599-3000
Criminal Justice
Army ROTC
Navy ROTC
Air Force ROTC

Florida Atlantic University
777 Glades Rd.
Boca Raton, FL 33431
(561) 367-3000
Air Force ROTC

Florida International University
University Park
Miami, FL 33199
(305) 348-2000
Criminal Justice
Army ROTC
Air Force ROTC

Florida Southern College
111 Lake Hollingsworth Dr.
Lakeland, FL 33801-5698
(941) 680-4111
Criminal Justice
Army ROTC

Florida State University
211 Westcott Bldg.
Tallahassee, FL 32306-1044
(904) 644-2525
Criminal Justice
Army ROTC
Navy ROTC
Air Force ROTC

Saint Thomas University
16400 NW 32nd Ave.
Miami, FL 33054
(305) 625-6000
Criminal Justice

Tampa College
3319 W Hillsborough Ave.
Tampa, FL 33614
(813) 879-6000
Criminal Justice

The University of West Florida
11000 University Pkwy.
Pensacola, FL 32514-5750
(904) 474-2000
Criminal Justice
Army ROTC

University of Central Florida
4000 Central Florida Blvd.
Orlando, FL 32816
(407) 823-2000
Criminal Justice
Army ROTC
Air Force ROTC

University of Florida
Gainesville, FL 32611
(904) 392-3261
Criminal Justice
Army ROTC
Navy ROTC
Air Force ROTC

University of Miami
University Station
Coral Gables, FL 33124
(305) 284-2211
Criminal Justice
Army ROTC
Air Force ROTC

University of North Florida
4567 St. Johns Bluff Rd. S
Jacksonville, FL 32224-2645
(904) 646-2666
Criminal Justice
Navy ROTC

University of South Florida
4202 Fowler Ave.
Tampa, FL 33620
(813) 974-2011
Criminal Justice
Army ROTC
Air Force ROTC

Georgia

Albany State University
504 College Dr.
Albany, GA 31705
(912) 439-4600
Criminal Justice
Army ROTC

Armstrong Atlantic State University
11935 Abercorn St.
Savannah, GA 31419
(912) 927-5211
Criminal Justice
Law
Army ROTC
Navy ROTC

Augusta State University
2500 Walton Way
Augusta, GA 30904-2200
(706) 737-1400
Criminal Justice
Army ROTC

Chattahoochee Technical Institute
980 S Cobb Dr.
Marietta, GA 30060-3398
(404) 528-4500
Criminal Justice

Columbus State University
4225 University Ave.
Columbus, GA 31907-5645
(706) 568-2001
Criminal Justice
Army ROTC

Floyd College
P.O. Box 1864
Rome, GA 30162-1864
(706) 802-5000
Criminal Justice

Fort Valley State University
1005 State College Dr.
Fort Valley, GA 31030-3298
(912) 825-6315
Criminal Justice
Army ROTC

Georgia Military College-Main
Campus
201 E Greene St.
Milledgeville, GA 31061-3398
(912) 454-2701
Criminal Justice

Georgia Southern University
Landrum Box 8033
Statesboro, GA 30460
(912) 681-5611
Criminal Justice
Army ROTC

Georgia State University
33 Gilmer St. SE
Atlanta, GA 30303-3083
(404) 651-2000
Criminal Justice
Army ROTC

Lagrange College
601 Broad St.
Lagrange, GA 30240
(706) 882-2911
Criminal Justice

Mercer University
1400 Coleman Ave.
Macon, GA 31207
(912) 752-2700
Criminal Justice
Army ROTC

Morris Brown College
643 Martin L. King, Jr. Dr.
Atlanta, GA 30314
(404) 220-0270
Criminal Justice
Navy ROTC

North Georgia College and State
University
College Ave.
Dahlonega, GA 30597
(706) 864-1600
Criminal Justice
Army ROTC

Reinhardt College
7300 Reinhardt College Pkwy.
Waleska, GA 30183
(770) 720-5600
Criminal Justice

Savannah Technical Institute
5717 White Bluff Rd.
Savannah, GA 31405-5594
(912) 351-6362
Criminal Justice

State University of West Georgia
1600 Maple St.
Carrollton, GA 30118-0001
(770) 836-6500
Criminal Justice
Army ROTC

University of Georgia
Athens, GA 30602
(706) 542-3030
Criminal Justice
Army ROTC
Air Force ROTC

Valdosta State University
North Patterson
Valdosta, GA 31698
(912) 333-5800
Criminal Justice
Air Force ROTC

Hawaii

Chaminade University of Honolulu
3140 Waialae Ave.
Honolulu, HI 96816
(808) 735-4711
Criminal Justice
Army ROTC
Air Force ROTC

Hawaii Pacific University
1164 Bishop St.
Honolulu, HI 96813
(808) 544-0200
Criminal Justice
Army ROTC
Air Force ROTC

Idaho

College of Southern Idaho
P.O. Box 1238
Twin Falls, ID 83301
(208) 733-9554
Criminal Justice

Idaho State University
741 S 7th Ave.
Pocatello, ID 83209
(208) 236-3215
Criminal Justice
Law

Lewis-Clark State College
500 8th Ave.
Lewiston, ID 83501
(208) 799-5272
Criminal Justice
Army ROTC

University of Idaho
Moscow, ID 83844-4140
(208) 885-6111
Criminal Justice
Army ROTC
Navy ROTC
Air Force ROTC

Illinois

Aurora University
347 S Gladstone Ave.
Aurora, IL 60506-4892
(630) 892-6431
Criminal Justice

Chicago State University
95th St. at King Dr.
Chicago, IL 60628
(312) 995-2000
Criminal Justice
Army ROTC

College of St. Francis
500 N Wilcox St.
Joliet, IL 60435
(815) 740-3360
Criminal Justice

Governors State University
1 University Pkwy.
University Park, IL 60466-0975
(708) 534-5000
Criminal Justice

Illinois State University
North and School St.
Normal, IL 617901000
(309) 438-2111
Criminal Justice
Army ROTC

Loyola University of Chicago
820 N Michigan Ave.
Chicago, IL 60611
(312) 915-6500
Criminal Justice
Army ROTC

Northeastern Illinois University
5500 N Saint Louis Ave.
Chicago, IL 60625
(312) 583-4050
Criminal Justice
Army ROTC
Air Force ROTC

Olivet Nazarene University
240 E Marsile
Bourbonnais, IL 60914
(815) 939-5011
Criminal Justice
Army ROTC

Quincy University
1800 College Ave.
Quincy, IL 62301-2699
(217) 222-8020
Criminal Justice

Saint Xavier University
3700 W 103rd St.
Chicago, IL 60655
(312) 298-3000
Criminal Justice
Corrections

University of Illinois at Chicago
601 S Morgan
Chicago, IL 60607
(312) 996-3000
Criminal Justice
Army ROTC
Air Force ROTC
Navy ROTC

Indiana
Anderson University
1100 E 5th St.
Anderson, IN 46012-3462
(317) 649-9071
Criminal Justice

Ball State University
2000 University Ave.
Muncie, IN 47306
(317) 289-1241
Criminal Justice
Corrections
Army ROTC

Calumet College of Saint Joseph
2400 New York Ave.
Whiting, IN 46394
(219) 473-7770
Criminal Justice

Indiana University at Bloomington
Bryan Hall
Bloomington, IN 47405
(812) 855-4848
Criminal Justice
Army ROTC
Air Force ROTC

Indiana Wesleyan University
4201 S Washington St.
Marion, IN 46953
(317) 674-6901
Criminal Justice

Martin University
P.O. Box 18567
Indianapolis, IN 46218
(317) 543-3235
Criminal Justice

Taylor University at Ft. Wayne
1025 W Rudisill Blvd.
Ft. Wayne, IN 46807
(219) 456-2111
Criminal Justice

Tri-State University
1 University Ave.
Angola, IN 46703-0307
(219) 665-4102
Criminal Justice
Law

Valparaiso University
U.S. Hwy. 30
Valparaiso, IN 46383-9978
(219) 464-5000
Criminal Justice

Iowa

Briar Cliff College
3303 Rebecca St.
Sioux City, IA 51104
(712) 279-5321
Criminal Justice

Graceland College
700 College Ave.
Lamoni, IA 50140
(515) 784-5000
Criminal Justice

Saint Ambrose University
518 W Locust St.
Davenport, IA 52803
(319) 333-6000
Criminal Justice

Simpson College
701 North C St.
Indianola, IA 50125
(515) 961-6251
Criminal Justice

Westmar University
1002 3rd Ave. SE
Le Mars, IA 51031
(712) 546-7081
Criminal Justice

Kansas

Friends University
2100 University
Wichita, KS 67213
(316) 261-5800
Criminal Justice

Highland Community College
P.O. Box 68
Highland, KS 66035-0068
(913) 442-6000
Criminal Justice

Kansas Wesleyan University
100 E Claflin
Salina, KS 67401-6196
(913) 827-5541
Criminal Justice

Ottawa University at Kansas City
10865 Grandview Ste. 2000
Overland Park, KS 66210
(913) 451-1431
Criminal Justice

Sterling College
Broadway and Cooper
Sterling, KS 67579
(316) 278-2173
Criminal Justice

Wichita State University
1845 Fairmount
Wichita, KS 67260
(316) 978-3456
Criminal Justice

Kentucky

Campbellsville University
1 University Dr.
Campbellsville, KY 42718-2799
(502) 789-5000
Criminal Justice

Kentucky Wesleyan College
3000 Frederica St.
P.O. Box 1039
Owensboro, KY 42302-1039
(502) 926-3111
Criminal Justice

Murray State University
P.O. Box 9
Murray, KY 420710009
(502) 762-3011
Criminal Justice
Army ROTC

Louisiana

Dillard University
2601 Gentilly Blvd.
New Orleans, LA 70122
(504) 283-8822
Criminal Justice
Army ROTC
Navy ROTC
Air Force ROTC

Grambling State University
P.O. Drawer 607 100 Main Floor
Grambling, LA 71245
(318) 247-3811
Criminal Justice
Law Enforcement/Police Science
Army ROTC
Air Force ROTC

Louisiana College
1140 College Dr.
Pineville, LA 71359
(318) 487-7011
Criminal Justice
Law Enforcement/Police Science

Louisiana St. Univ. & Agrl. & Mech. &
Hebert Laws Ctr.
Baton Rouge, LA 70803
(504) 388-3202
Criminal Justice
Army ROTC
Air Force ROTC

Louisiana State
University-Shreveport
1 University Pl.
Shreveport, LA 71115-2399
(318) 797-5000
Criminal Justice
Army ROTC

Mcneese State University
4100 Ryan Floor
Lake Charles, LA 70609
(318) 475-5000
Criminal Justice
Army ROTC

Northeast Louisiana University
700 University Ave.
Monroe, LA 71209
(318) 342-1000
Criminal Justice
Law Enforcement/Police Science
Army ROTC

Southeastern Louisiana University
100 W Dakota
Hammond, LA 70402
(504) 549-2000
Criminal Justice
Law Enforcement/Police Science
Army ROTC

Southern University at New Orleans
6400 Press Dr.
New Orleans, LA 70126
(504) 286-5000
Criminal Justice
Army ROTC

Tulane University of Louisiana
6823 St. Charles Ave.
New Orleans, LA 70118
(504) 865-5000
Criminal Justice
Army ROTC
Navy ROTC
Air Force ROTC

University of Southwestern
Louisiana
104 University Cir.
Lafayette, LA 70503
(318) 482-1000
Criminal Justice
Law Enforcement/Police Science
Army ROTC

Maine

Andover College
901 Washington Ave.
Portland, ME 04103
(207) 774-6126
Criminal Justice

University of Maine at Augusta
46 University Dr.
Augusta, ME 04330-9410
(207) 621-3146
Criminal Justice
Law Enforcement/Police Science

Massachusetts

American International College
1000 State Floor
Springfield, MA 01109
(413) 737-7000
Criminal Justice

Anna Maria College
10 Sunset Ln.
Paxton, MA 01612-1198
(508) 849-3300
Criminal Justice

Becker College at Worcester
61 Sever Floor
Worcester, MA 01615-0071
(508) 791-9241
Criminal Justice

Berkshire Community College
1350 West St.
Pittsfield, MA 01201-5786
(413) 499-4660
Criminal Justice

Boston University
145 Bay State Rd.
Boston, MA 02215
(617) 353-2000
Criminal Justice
Army ROTC
Navy ROTC
Air Force ROTC

Cape Cod Community College
2240 Iyanough Rd.
West Barnstable, MA 02668-1599
(508) 362-2131
Criminal Justice

Middlesex Community College
Springs Rd.
Bedford, MA 01730
(508) 656-3200
Criminal Justice

Mount Wachusett Community
College
444 Green Floor
Gardner, MA 01440
(508) 632-6600
Criminal Justice
Corrections

Newbury College Inc
129 Fisher Ave.
Brookline, MA 02146
(617) 730-7000
Criminal Justice

North Shore Community College
1 Ferncroft Rd.
Danvers, MA 01923
(508) 762-4000
Criminal Justice
Law Enforcement/Police Science

Northeastern University
360 Huntington Ave.
Boston, MA 02115
(617) 373-2000
Criminal Justice
Corrections
Law Enforcement/Police Science
Army ROTC

Northern Essex Community College
Elliott Way
Haverhill, MA 01830-2399
(508) 374-3900
Criminal Justice

Quincy College
34 Coddington St.
Quincy, MA 02169
(617) 984-1600
Criminal Justice

University of Massachusetts at Boston
100 Morrissey Blvd.
Boston, MA 02125-3393
(617) 287-6000
Criminal Justice

University of Massachusetts at Lowell
1 University Ave.
Lowell, MA 01854
(508) 934-4000
Criminal Justice
Army ROTC
Air Force ROTC

Western New England College
1215 Wilbraham Rd.
Springfield, MA 01119
(413) 782-3111
Criminal Justice
Law Enforcement/Police Science
Army ROTC
Air Force ROTC

Westfield State College
Western Ave.
Westfield, MA 01086
(413) 568-3311
Criminal Justice
Army ROTC

Michigan
Delta College
University Center
University Center, MI 48710
(517) 686-9000
Criminal Justice
Corrections
Law Enforcement/Police Science

Lansing Community College
419 N Capitol Ave.
Lansing, MI 48901-7210
(517) 483-1957
Criminal Justice
Law Enforcement/Police Science

Madonna University
36600 Schoolcraft Rd.
Livonia, MI 48150
(313) 432-5300
Criminal Justice

Michigan State University
East Lansing, MI 48824
(517) 355-1855
Criminal Justice
Law Enforcement/Police Science
Army ROTC
Air Force ROTC

Muskegon Community College
221 S Quarterline Rd.
Muskegon, MI 49442
(616) 777-0311
Criminal Justice
Corrections

Northern Michigan University
1401 Presque Isle
Marquette, MI 49855
(906) 227-1000
Criminal Justice
Law Enforcement/Police Science
Army ROTC

Saginaw Valley State University
7400 Bay Rd.
University Center, MI 48710
(517) 790-4055
Criminal Justice

Schoolcraft College
18600 Haggerty Rd.
Livonia, MI 48152
(313) 462-4400
Criminal Justice
Law Enforcement/Police Science

Siena Heights College
1247 Siena Heights Dr.
Adrian, MI 49221
(517) 263-0731
Criminal Justice

Law Enforcement/Police Science
University of Detroit Mercy
P.O. Box 19900
Detroit, MI 48219-0900
(313) 993-1000
Criminal Justice

Wayne State University
656 W Kirby
Detroit, MI 48202
(313) 577-2424
Criminal Justice
Army ROTC

Minnesota

Bemidji State University
1500 Birchmont Dr.
Bemidji, MN 56601
(800) 475-2001
Criminal Justice
Army ROTC

Moorhead State University
1104 7th Ave. S
Moorhead, MN 56563
(218) 236-2011
Criminal Justice
Army ROTC
Air Force ROTC

Saint Cloud State University
720 4th Ave. S
St. Cloud, MN 563014498
(320) 255-0121
Criminal Justice
Army ROTC

Saint Mary's University of Minnesota
700 Terrace Hts.
Winona, MN 55987-1399
(507) 452-4430
Criminal Justice

Mississippi

Alcorn State University
P.O. Box 359
Lorman, MS 39096
(601) 877-6100
Criminal Justice
Army ROTC

Coahoma Community College
3240 Friars Point Rd.
Clarksdale, MS 38614
(601) 627-2571
Criminal Justice

Delta State University
Kethley 202
Cleveland, MS 38733
(601) 846-4000
Criminal Justice
Army ROTC
Air Force ROTC

Jackson State University
1440 J. R. Lynch Floor
Jackson, MS 39217
(601) 968-2272
Criminal Justice
Army ROTC

Meridian Community College
910 Hwy. 19 N
Meridian, MS 39307
(601) 483-8241
Criminal Justice
Corrections

Mississippi Gulf Coast Community
College
Central Office P.O. Box 67
Perkinston, MS 39573
(601) 928-5211
Criminal Justice

Mississippi Valley State University
14000 Hwy. 82 W
Itta Bena, MS 38941-1400
(601) 254-9041
Criminal Justice
Army ROTC
Air Force ROTC

Northeast Mississippi Community
College
Cunningham Blvd.
Booneville, MS 38829
(601) 728-7751
Criminal Justice

University of Southern Mississippi
2901 Hardy St. Box 5001
Hattiesburg, MS 39406
(601) 266-4111
Criminal Justice
Army ROTC
Air Force ROTC

Missouri
Columbia College
1001 Rogers
Columbia, MO 65216
(573) 875-8700
Criminal Justice
Law Enforcement/Police Science
Army ROTC
Navy ROTC
Air Force ROTC

Hannibal-Lagrange College
2800 Palmyra Rd.
Hannibal, MO 63401
(314) 221-3675
Criminal Justice

Harris-Stowe State College
3026 Laclede Ave.
St. Louis, MO 63103-2136
(314) 340-3366
Criminal Justice

Lindenwood College
209 S Kingshighway
St. Charles, MO 63301
(314) 949-2000
Criminal Justice

Missouri Valley College
500 E. College St.
Marshall, MO 65340
(816) 831-4000
Criminal Justice

Missouri Western State College
4525 Downs Dr.
St. Joseph, MO 64507
(816) 271-4200
Law Enforcement/Police Science
Criminal Justice
Army ROTC

Montana
Fort Peck Community College
P.O. Box 398
Poplar, MT 59255
(406) 768-5551
Criminal Justice

University of Great Falls
1301 Twentieth St. S
Great Falls, MT 59405-4996
(406) 761-8210
Criminal Justice

University of Great Falls
1301 Twentieth St. S
Great Falls, MT 59405-4996
(406) 761-8210
Criminal Justice

Nebraska
University of Nebraska at Kearney
905 W 25th St.
Kearney, NE 68849-1212
(308) 865-8441
Criminal Justice

University of Nebraska at Omaha
60th and Dodge St.
Omaha, NE 68182
(402) 554-2800
Criminal Justice
Army ROTC

New Hampshire
Wayne State College
1111 Main St.
Wayne, NE 68787
(402) 375-7000
Criminal Justice
Army ROTC

Nevada
University of Nevada at Las Vegas
4505 S Maryland Pky.
Las Vegas, NV 89154
(702) 895-3011
Criminal Justice
Army ROTC

Western Nevada Community College
2201 W College Pky.
Carson City, NV 89703
(702) 887-3000
Criminal Justice

New Hampshire
Hesser College
3 Sundial Ave.
Manchester, NH 03103
(603) 668-6660
Criminal Justice

Mcintosh College
23 Cataract Ave.
Dover, NH 03820
(603) 742-3518
Criminal Justice

New England College
7 Main St.
Henniker, NH 03242
(603) 428-2211
Criminal Justice

Saint Anselm College
100 St. Anselm Dr. Ste. 1729
Manchester, NH 03102-1310
(603) 641-7000
Criminal Justice
Army ROTC
Air Force ROTC

New Jersey
Jersey City State College
2039 Kennedy Blvd.
Jersey City, NJ 07305
(201) 200-2000
Criminal Justice
Corrections

Monmouth University
185 Hwy. 35
West Long Branch, NJ 07764
(908) 571-3400
Criminal Justice

Rutgers University at Newark
Newark Campus
Newark, NJ 07102
(201) 648-1766
Criminal Justice

Seton Hall University
400 S Orange Ave.
South Orange, NJ 07079
(201) 761-9000
Criminal Justice
Army ROTC

New Mexico
Albuquerque Technical Vocational
Institute
525 Buena Vista SE
Albuquerque, NM 87106
(505) 224-3000
Criminal Justice

Northern New Mexico Community
College
1002 N Onate Floor
Espanola, NM 87532
(505) 747-2100
Criminal Justice

Santa Fe Community College
S Richards Ave. P.O.B. 4187
Santa Fe, NM 87502-4187
(505) 471-8200
Criminal Justice
Corrections

Univerity of New Mexico at Gallup
200 College Rd.
Gallup, NM 87301
(505) 863-7500
Criminal Justice
Corrections

Western New Mexico University
1000 College Ave.
Silver City, NM 88061
(505) 538-6336
Criminal Justice

New York
Columbia-Greene Community College
4400 Rte. 23
Hudson, NY 12534
(518) 828-4181
Criminal Justice

Long Island University at C.W. Post
Northern Blvd.
Greenvale, NY 11548
(516) 299-2413,
Criminal Justice
Army ROTC
Air Force ROTC

Mercy College-Main Campus
555 Broadway
Dobbs Ferry, NY 10522
(914) 693-4500
Criminal Justice
Law Enforcement/Police Science
Army ROTC
Air Force ROTC

Rochester Institute of Technology
1 Lomb Memorial Dr.
Rochester, NY 14623-5603
(716) 475-2411
Criminal Justice
Army ROTC
Air Force ROTC

Saint John's University at New York
8000 Utopia Pwy
Jamaica, NY 11439
(718) 990-6161
Criminal Justice
Army ROTC
Air Force ROTC

Saint Thomas Aquinas College
125 Rte. 340
Sparkill, NY 10976
(914) 398-4000
Criminal Justice
Air Force ROTC

SUNY at Albany
1400 Washington Ave.
Albany, NY 12222
(518) 442-3300
Criminal Justice
Army ROTC
Navy ROTC
Air Force ROTC

SUNY College at Brockport
350 New Campus Dr.
Brockport, NY 14420
(716) 395-2211
Criminal Justice
Army ROTC

SUNY College at Buffalo
1300 Elmwood Ave.
Buffalo, NY 14222
(716) 878-4000
Criminal Justice

SUNY College at Oswego
Oswego, NY 13126
(315) 341-2500
Criminal Justice
Army ROTC

SUNY College at Plattsburgh
Plattsburgh, NY 12901
(518) 564-2000
Criminal Justice

North Carolina
Guilford College
5800 W Friendly Ave.
Greensboro, NC 27410
(910) 316-2000
Criminal Justice

Livingstone College
701 W Monroe Floor
Salisbury, NC 28144
(704) 638-5500
Criminal Justice
Army ROTC

Methodist College
5400 Ramsey Floor
Fayetteville, NC 28311
(910) 630-7000
Criminal Justice
Army ROTC
Air Force ROTC

Pfeiffer University
Hwy. 52
Misenheimer, NC 28109-0960
(704) 463-1360
Criminal Justice
Army ROTC

Shaw University
118 E South Floor
Raleigh, NC 27601
(919) 546-8200
Criminal Justice
Army ROTC

North Dakota
Minot State University
500 University Ave. W
Minot, ND 58707
(701) 858-3340
Criminal Justice

University of North Dakota-Main
Campus
University Station
Grand Forks, ND 58202
(701) 777-4463
Criminal Justice
Army ROTC

Ohio
Bowling Green State
University-Firelands
901 Rye Beach Rd.
Huron, OH 44839
(419) 433-5560
Criminal Justice

Bowling Green State University-Main
Campus
220 McFall Ctr.
Bowling Green, OH 43403
(419) 372-2531
Criminal Justice
Army ROTC
Air Force ROTC

Defiance College
701 N Clinton
Defiance, OH 43512
(419) 784-4010
Criminal Justice

Kent State University at Main Campus
Kent, OH 44242-0001
(330) 672-3000
Criminal Justice
Corrections
Army ROTC
Air Force ROTC

Ohio Dominican College
1216 Sunbury Rd.
Columbus, OH 43219
(614) 253-2741
Criminal Justice

The Union Institute
440 E Mcmillan Floor
Cincinnati, OH 45206-1925
(800) 486-3116
Criminal Justice

University of Dayton
300 College Park
Dayton, OH 45469
(513) 229-4122
Criminal Justice
Corrections
Law Enforcement/Police Science
Army ROTC

University of Toledo
2801 W Bancroft
Toledo, OH 43606
(419) 530-2696
Criminal Justice
Law Enforcement/Police Science
Air Force ROTC

Xavier University
3800 Victory Pkwy.
Cincinnati, OH 45207-1092
(513) 745-3000
Criminal Justice
Corrections
Army ROTC

Youngstown State University
410 Wick Ave.
Youngstown, OH 44555
(330) 742-3000
Criminal Justice
Law Enforcement/Police Science
Army ROTC

Oklahoma
East Central University
12th & Francis
Ada, OK 748206899
(405) 332-8000
Criminal Justice
Army ROTC

Northeastern State University
600 North Grand
Tahlequah, OK 74464-2399
(918) 456-5511
Criminal Justice
Army ROTC

Southeastern Oklahoma State
University
P.O. Box 4137
Durant, OK 74701
(405) 924-0121
Criminal Justice

Southern Nazarene University
6729 NW 39th Expy.
Bethany, OK 73008
(405) 789-6400
Criminal Justice

Southwestern Oklahoma State
University
100 Campus Dr.
Weatherford, OK 73096-3098
(405) 772-6611
Criminal Justice

University of Central Oklahoma
100 N University Dr.
Edmond, OK 73034
(405) 341-2980
Criminal Justice
Army ROTC

Oregon

Blue Mountain Community College
P.O. Box 100
Pendleton, OR 97801
(503) 276-1260
Criminal Justice
Law Enforcement/Police Science

Chemeketa Community College
P.O. Box 14007
Salem, OR 97309-7070
(503) 399-5000
Criminal Justice

Portland Community College
P.O. Box 19000
Portland, OR 97280-0990
(503) 244-6111
Criminal Justice

Portland State University
P.O. Box 751
Portland, OR 97207-0751
(503) 725-4433
Criminal Justice
Army ROTC

Southern Oregon State College
1250 Siskiyou Blvd.
Ashland, OR 97520
(541) 552-6327
Criminal Justice
Army ROTC

Southwestern Oregon Community
College
1988 Newmark Ave.
Coos Bay, OR 97420
(541) 888-2525
Criminal Justice

Western Oregon State College
345 N Monmouth Ave.
Monmouth, OR 97361
(503) 838-8000
Criminal Justice
Army ROTC

Pennsylvania

Allentown College of Saint Francis
De Sales
2755 Station Ave.
Center Valley, PA 18034-9568
(610) 282-1100
Criminal Justice
Army ROTC

Chatham College
Woodland Rd.
Pittsburgh, PA 15232
(412) 365-1100
Criminal Justice

Duquesne University
Administration Bldg. 600 Forbes Ave.
Pittsburgh, PA 15282
(412) 396-6000
Criminal Justice
Army ROTC

Edinboro University of Pennsylvania
Edinboro, PA 16444
(814) 732-2000
Criminal Justice
Law Enforcement/Police Science
Army ROTC

Elizabethtown College
One Alpha Dr.
Elizabethtown, PA 17022
(717) 361-1000
Criminal Justice

Gannon University
109 W Sixth Floor
Erie, PA 16541
(814) 871-7000
Criminal Justice
Army ROTC

Holy Family College
Grant and Frankford Ave.
Philadelphia, PA 19114-2094
(215) 637-7700
Criminal Justice

King's College
133 N River Floor
Wilkes Barre, PA 18711
(717) 826-5900
Criminal Justice
Army ROTC
Air Force ROTC

Kutztown University of Pennsylvania
Kutztown, PA 19530
(215) 683-4000
Criminal Justice
Army ROTC

La Salle University
1900 W Olney Ave.
Philadelphia, PA 19141-1199
(215) 951-1000
Criminal Justice
Army ROTC
Air Force ROTC

Lackawanna Junior College
501 Vine Floor
Scranton, PA 18509
(717) 961-7810
Criminal Justice
Army ROTC

Lincoln University
Lincoln University, PA 19352
(610) 932-8300
Criminal Justice

Pennsylvania State
University-Harrisburg Capital
777 W Harrisburg Pike
Middletown, PA 17057
(717) 948-600
Criminal Justice

Pennsylvania State University at Main
Campus
201 Old Main
University Park, PA 16802
(814) 865-4700
Criminal Justice
Army ROTC
Navy ROTC
Air Force ROTC

Shippensburg University of
Pennsylvania
1871 Old Main Dr.
Shippensburg, PA 17257-2299
(717) 532-9121
Criminal Justice
Army ROTC

Temple University
Broad and Montgomery
Philadelphia, PA 19122
(215) 204-7000
Criminal Justice
Army ROTC

University of Scranton
Linden and Monroe
Scranton, PA 18510
(717) 941-7400
Criminal Justice
Army ROTC
Air Force ROTC

Villanova University
800 Lancaster Ave.
Villanova, PA 19085-1699
(610) 519-4500
Criminal Justice
Army ROTC
Navy ROTC
Air Force ROTC

West Chester University of
Pennsylvania
University Ave. & High St.
West Chester, PA 19383
(610) 436-1000
Criminal Justice

Rhode Island

Rhode Island College
600 Mount Pleasant Ave.
Providence, RI 02908
(401) 456-8000
Criminal Justice
Army ROTC

Salve Regina University
100 Ochre Pt. Ave.
Newport, RI 02840-4192
(401) 847-6650
Criminal Justice
Army ROTC

South Carolina

Aiken Technical College
P.O. Drawer 696
Aiken, SC 29802
(803) 593-9231
Criminal Justice

Central Carolina Technical College
506 N Guignard Dr.
Sumter, SC 29150
(803) 778-1961
Criminal Justice

Charleston Southern University
9200 University Blvd.
Charleston, SC 29406
(803) 863-7000
Criminal Justice
Air Force ROTC

Chesterfield-Marlboro Technical
College
Drawer 1007 1201 Chesterfield Hwy.
Cheraw, SC
Criminal Justice

Denmark Technical College
P.O. Box 327
Denmark, SC 29042
(803) 793-5149
Criminal Justice

Florence Darlington Technical
College
P.O. Box 100548
Florence, SC 29501-0548
(803) 661-8324
Criminal Justice

Greenville Technical College
P.O. Box 5616 Station B
Greenville, SC 29606-5616
(864) 25
Criminal Justice

Horry-Georgetown Technical
College
P.O. Box 1966
Conway, SC 29526
(803) 347-3186
Criminal Justice

Midlands Technical College
P.O. Box 2408
Columbia, SC 29202
(803) 738-8324
Criminal Justice

Orangeburg Calhoun Technical
College
3250 Saint Matthews Rd.
Orangeburg, SC 29115
(803) 536-0311
Criminal Justice

Piedmont Technical College
P.O. Drawer 1467
Greenwood, SC 29648
(864) 941-8324
Criminal Justice

Technical College of the
Lowcountry
921 S Ribaut Rd.
Beaufort, SC 29901
(803) 525-8324
Criminal Justice

Tri-County Technical College
P.O. Box 587
Pendleton, SC 29670
(864) 646-8361
Criminal Justice

Trident Technical College
P.O. Box 118067
Charleston, SC 29423-8067
(803) 572-6111
Criminal Justice

Williamsburg Technical College
601 Martin Luther King Jr. Ave.
Kingstree, SC 29556
(803) 354-2021
Criminal Justice

South Dakota
Huron University
333 9th St. SW
Huron, SD 57350
(605) 352-8721
Criminal Justice

Mount Marty College
1105 W 8th St.
Yankton, SD 57078
(605) 668-1011
Criminal Justice
Army ROTC

Oglala Lakota College
Box 490
Kyle, SD 57752
(605) 455-2321
Criminal Justice

University of South Dakota
414 E Clark Floor
Vermillion, SD 57069-2390
(605) 677-5011
Criminal Justice
Army ROTC

Tennessee
Belmont University
1900 Belmont Blvd.
Nashville, TN 37212-3757
(615) 460-6000
Criminal Justice

Lane College
545 Lane Ave.
Jackson, TN 38301
(901) 426-7500
Criminal Justice

Texas
Angelo State University
2601 West Ave. N
San Angelo, TX 76909
(915) 942-2017
Criminal Justice
Air Force ROTC

Bee County College
3800 Charco Rd.
Beeville, TX 78102
(512) 358-3130
Criminal Justice
Corrections
Law Enforcement/Police Science

Blinn College
902 College Ave.
Brenham, TX 77833
(409) 830-4000
Criminal Justice

Brazosport College
500 College Dr.
Lake Jackson, TX 77566
(409) 266-3000
Criminal Justice
Law Enforcement/Police Science

College of The Mainland
1200 Amburn Rd.
Texas City, TX 77591
(409) 938-1211
Criminal Justice

Dallas Baptist University
3000 Mountain Creek Pkwy.
Dallas, TX 75211
(214) 333-7100
Criminal Justice
Corrections

Del Mar College
101 Baldwin
Corpus Christi, TX 78404-3897
(512) 886-1255
Criminal Justice
Law Enforcement/Police Science

El Centro College
Main and Lamar
Dallas, TX 75202
(214) 860-2037
Criminal Justice

Galveston College
4015 Ave. Q
Galveston, TX 77550
(409) 763-6551
Criminal Justice

Hill College
P.O. Box 619
Hillsboro, TX 76645
(817) 582-2555
Criminal Justice

Kilgore College
1100 Broadway
Kilgore, TX 75662-3299
(903) 984-8531
Criminal Justice
Law Enforcement/Police Science

Lamar University-Beaumont
P.O. Box 10001
Beaumont, TX 77710
(409) 880-7011
Criminal Justice
Law Enforcement/Police Science
Army ROTC

McLennan Community College
1400 College Dr.
Waco, TX 76708
(817) 299-8000
Criminal Justice
Corrections

McMurry University
S 14th and Sayles Blvd.
Abilene, TX 79697
(915) 691-6200
Criminal Justice
Army ROTC

Midland College
3600 N Garfield
Midland, TX 79705
(915) 685-4500
Criminal Justice
Law Enforcement/Police Science

Midwestern State University
3410 Taft Blvd.
Wichita Falls, TX 76308-2099
(817) 689-4000
Criminal Justice

North Harris Montgomery Community
College District
250 N Sam Houston Pkwy. E, Ste. 300
Houston, TX 77060
(713) 591-3500
Criminal Justice
Law Enforcement/Police Science

St. Edwards University
3001 S Congress Ave.
Austin, TX 787046489
(512) 448-8400
Criminal Justice

Sam Houston State University
P.O. Box 2026
Huntsville, TX 77341
(409) 294-1111
Criminal Justice
Corrections
Law Enforcement/Police Science
Army ROTC

Southwest Texas State University
601 University Dr.
San Marcos, TX 78666
(512) 245-2111
Criminal Justice
Corrections
Law Enforcement/Police Science
Army ROTC
Air Force ROTC

Stephen F. Austin State University
1936 North Floor
Nacogdoches, TX 75962
(409) 468-3806
Criminal Justice
Corrections
Law Enforcement/Police Science
Army ROTC

Sul Ross State University
Alpine, TX 79832
(915) 837-8011
Criminal Justice

Tarleton State University
Tarleton Station
Stephenville, TX 76402
(817) 968-9000
Criminal Justice
Army ROTC

Tarrant County Junior College
1500 Houston Floor
Ft Worth, TX 76102
(817) 336-7851
Criminal Justice
Law Enforcement/Police Science

Temple College
2600 S 1st Floor
Temple, TX 76504-7435
(817) 773-9961
Criminal Justice

Texas A & M University-Corpus Christi
6300 Ocean Dr.
Corpus Christi, TX 78412
(512) 994-5700
Criminal Justice
Army ROTC

Texas A&M University-Commerce
E Texas Station
Commerce, TX 75429
(903) 886-5081
Criminal Justice

Texas Christian University
2800 S University Dr.
Ft Worth, TX 76129
(817) 921-7000
Criminal Justice
Army ROTC
Air Force ROTC

Texas Southmost College
80 Fort Brown
Brownsville, TX 78520
(210) 544-8200
Criminal Justice
Law Enforcement/Police Science

Texas Wesleyan University
1201 Wesleyan Floor
Ft Worth, TX 76105-1536
(817) 531-4444
Criminal Justice
Army ROTC
Air Force ROTC

Texas Woman's University
Box 425587
Denton, TX 76204-5587
(817) 898-2000
Criminal Justice

The University of Texas at Arlington
701 S Nedderman Dr.
Arlington, TX 76019
(817) 272-2011
Criminal Justice
Army ROTC
Air Force ROTC

The University of Texas at El Paso
500 W University Ave.
El Paso, TX 79968
(915) 747-5000
Criminal Justice
Army ROTC
Air Force ROTC

The University of Texas at San
Antonio
6900 N Loop 1604 W
San Antonio, TX 78249-0616
(210) 458-4011
Criminal Justice
Army ROTC
Air Force ROTC

The University of Texas at Tyler
3900 University Blvd.
Tyler, TX 75701-6699
(906) 566-7103
Criminal Justice

University of Central Texas
P.O. Box 1416
Killeen, TX 76540-1416
(817) 526-8262
Criminal Justice
Army ROTC

University of Houston-Victoria
2506 E Red River
Victoria, TX 77901
(512) 576-3151
Criminal Justice

University of Mary Hardin Baylor
M H-B Station
Belton, TX 76513
(817) 939-8642
Criminal Justice
Air Force ROTC

Vernon Regional Junior College
4400 College Dr.
Vernon, TX 76384-4092
(817) 552-6291
Criminal Justice

Utah
Dixie College
225 S 700 E
St. George, UT 84770
(801) 652-7500
Criminal Justice

Salt Lake Community College
P.O. Box 30808
Salt Lake City, UT 84130
(801) 967-4082
Criminal Justice
Army ROTC
Air Force ROTC

Snow College
150 E College Ave.
Ephraim, UT 84627
(801) 283-4021
Criminal Justice

Southern Utah University
351 West Ctr.
Cedar City, UT 84720
(801) 586-7700
Criminal Justice
Law Enforcement/Police Science

Weber State University
3750 Harrison Blvd.
Ogden, UT 84408
(801) 626-6000
Criminal Justice
Law Enforcement/Police Science
Army ROTC
Navy ROTC
Air Force ROTC

Vermont
Castleton State College
Castleton, VT 05735
(802) 468-5611
Criminal Justice

Virginia
Bluefield College
3000 College Dr.
Bluefield, VA 24605
(540) 326-3682
Criminal Justice

Radford University
Norwood Floor
Radford, VA 24142
(540) 831-5000
Criminal Justice
Army ROTC

Roanoke College
221 College Ln.
Salem, VA 24153
(540) 375-2500
Criminal Justice

Saint Pauls College
115 College Dr.
Lawrenceville, VA 23868
(804) 848-3111
Criminal Justice
Army ROTC

University of Richmond
Maryland Hall
Richmond, VA 23173
(804) 289-8000
Criminal Justice
Army ROTC

Washington

Bellevue Community College
3000 Landerholm Cir. SE
Bellevue, WA 98007-6484
(206) 641-0111
Criminal Justice

Central Washington University
400 E 8th
Ellensburg, WA 98926
(509) 963-2111
Criminal Justice
Army ROTC
Air Force ROTC

Clark College
1800 E Mcloughlin Blvd.
Vancouver, WA 98663
(360) 992-2000
Criminal Justice

Columbia Basin College
2600 N 20th Ave.
Pasco, WA 99301
(509) 547-0511
Criminal Justice

Eastern Washington University
Cheney, WA 99004-2496
(509) 359-6200
Criminal Justice
Army ROTC

Everett Community College
801 Wetmore Ave.
Everett, WA 98201
(206) 388-9100
Criminal Justice

Gonzaga University
E 502 Boone Ave.
Spokane, WA 99258-0001
(509) 328-4220
Criminal Justice
Army ROTC

Highline Community College
P.O. Box 98000
Des Moines, WA 98198-9800
(206) 878-3710
Criminal Justice

Lower Columbia College
P.O. Box 3010
Longview, WA 98632
(360) 577-2311
Criminal Justice

Peninsula College
1502 E Lauridsen Blvd.
Port Angeles, WA 98362
(360) 452-9277
Criminal Justice

Pierce College
9401 Farwest Dr. SW
Lakewood, WA 98498
(206) 964-6500
Criminal Justice

Seattle University
12th and Columbia
Seattle, WA 98122
(206) 296-6000
Criminal Justice
Army ROTC
Navy ROTC
Air Force ROTC

Shoreline Community College
16101 Greenwood Ave. N
Seattle, WA 98133
(206) 546-4101
Criminal Justice

Tacoma Community College
5900 S 12th Floor
Tacoma, WA 98465
(206) 566-5000
Criminal Justice
Corrections

Walla Walla Community College
500 Tausick Way
Walla Walla, WA 99362
(509) 522-2500
Criminal Justice

Whatcom Community College
237 W Kellogg Rd.
Bellingham, WA 98226
(360) 676-2170
Criminal Justice

Yakima Valley Community College
P.O. Box 1647
Yakima, WA 98907
(509) 574-4600
Criminal Justice

West Virginia
Bluefield State College
219 Rock Floor
Bluefield, WV 24701
(304) 327-4000
Criminal Justice
Law Enforcement/Police Science

Fairmont State College
1201 Locust Ave.
Fairmont, WV 26554
(304) 367-4000
Criminal Justice
Law Enforcement/Police Science
Army ROTC

Marshall University
400 Hal Greer Blvd.
Huntington, WV 25755
(304) 696-6690
Criminal Justice
Law Enforcement/Police Science
Army ROTC

Salem-Teikyo University
223 W Main Floor
Salem, WV 26426
(304) 782-5389
Army ROTC
Air Force ROTC

Southern West Virginia Community
and Technical College
Box 2900
Mt. Gay, WV 25637
(304) 792-7098
Criminal Justice

The College of West Virginia
500 S Kanawha Floor
Beckley, WV 25802
(304) 253-7351
Criminal Justice
Corrections

West Liberty State College
West Liberty, WV 26074
(304) 336-5000
Criminal Justice

West Virginia State College
Rte. 25
Institute, WV 25112
(304) 766-3000
Criminal Justice
Law Enforcement/Police Science
Army ROTC

West Virginia University at
Parkersburg
Rte. 5, Box 167a
Parkersburg, WV 26101
(304) 424-8000
Criminal Justice

Wheeling Jesuit University
316 Washington Ave.
Wheeling, WV 26003
(304) 243-2000
Criminal Justice

Wisconsin
Carroll College
100 N East Ave.
Waukesha, WI 53186
(414) 547-1211
Criminal Justice

Edgewood College
855 Woodrow
Madison, WI 53711
(608) 257-4861
Criminal Justice

Marquette University
615 N 11th Floor
Milwaukee, WI 53233
(414) 288-7710
Criminal Justice
Army ROTC
Navy ROTC
Air Force ROTC

Mount Senario College
1500 College Ave. W
Ladysmith, WI 54848
(715) 532-5511
Criminal Justice

University of Wisconsin-Eau Claire
Park and Garfield
Eau Claire, WI 54701
(715) 836-2637
Criminal Justice

University of Wisconsin-Milwaukee
P.O. Box 413
Milwaukee, WI 53201
(414) 229-4444
Criminal Justice
Army ROTC

University of Wisconsin-Oshkosh
800 Algoma Blvd.
Oshkosh, WI 54901
(414) 424-1234
Criminal Justice
Army ROTC

University of Wisconsin-Platteville
1 University Plz.
Platteville, WI 53818
(608) 342-1421
Criminal Justice
Army ROTC

Wyoming
Casper College
125 College Dr.
Casper, WY 82601
(307) 268-2110
Criminal Justice

Central Wyoming College
2660 Peck Ave.
Riverton, WY 82501
(307) 855-2000
Criminal Justice

Eastern Wyoming College
3200 West C St.
Torrington, WY 82240
(307) 532-8200
Criminal Justice

THE INSIDE TRACK

Who:	Frank Marousek
What:	Assistant Dean of Admissions
Where:	John Jay College of Criminal Justice, New York City
How long:	Over 19 years with the New York City Police Department, after serving in the Army's Military Police.
Degree:	Bachelor's degree at John Jay College; Master's degree at New York University

Insider's Advice

I strongly recommend that students pursue an associate degree or a bachelor's degree in a field related to criminal justice—either in pure criminal justice, police science, government, or another discipline. At John Jay, many of our students study forensic psychology and deviant behavior and social control. A college education is very important. For example, many students who attend John Jay aspire to go into the Bureau (FBI) and they don't realize what a long path that is. They still need several years of work experience in addition to a bachelor's degree before they can even take the Federal exam for the Bureau. Having a master's degree lowers that requirement somewhat.

It's important to get a degree, too, because there are some things that you just can't learn on the job. I ran into one of our graduates recently at a reunion who had completed our master's degree program in criminal justice. I asked him what he had learned through the program that was most important to him now. He said, bar none, that the ability to conduct sound research was the most important part of what he had learned. He is currently in a supervisory position in a unit that conducts research into things like shootings, etc. There are some things you just have to learn in an academic environment.

Insider's Take on the Future

What you get your degree in depends on your individual interests. Our students aren't lock-stepped into an area of specialization right away. Our liberal arts and introductory courses delve into every aspect of a field, so by the time students are ready to specialize, they have a good idea of the specific area of study on which to concentrate. Students don't go directly into something like law enforcement administration or police science. We've designed our majors this way because we have people who are already in the law enforcement field who are returning to college to pursue areas that are germane to their career development. We also have students who have never worked in the field, but are seeking careers in law enforcement.

A military background offers great educational benefits. We see people coming out of the military after a three-year stint with a sizable amount of money to go to school. The military has several programs to help you get an education. Recently, the National Guard in New York state developed a program where they give their members free tuition if they attend a state college or university.

CHAPTER | 4

This chapter will give you an idea of how much an education will cost, according to which school or training program you choose; what kind of financial aid is available to help with expenses; and where you need to go to find that funding. You'll also find information on scholarship programs geared especially toward law enforcement students.

FINANCIAL AID FOR THE TRAINING YOU NEED

Mention money and college in the same sentence and most people reach for the antacids. The funny thing is, it's not as bad as you think. The Department of Education, in their very helpful publication *The Study Guide*, cites the results of a recent Gallup poll surveying 13- to 21-year-olds about the average cost of public education in two- and four-year colleges. It turns out that the people who were surveyed guessed the costs to be three times higher than they actually are. Their estimates for four-year private colleges weren't much better—they guessed the costs to be one-third higher than they are in reality.

That's not to say that a college education is cheap; some colleges can be *very* expensive. But even those institutions aren't necessarily out of reach if you are willing to look into financial aid prospects. This will take a bit of time and effort on your part, of course, but it'll all be worth it when you find that perfect financial break.

EXPENSES TO EXPECT

The two most expensive elements of a college education are tuition and fees. Institutions will charge to teach you and to let you use their facilities—they call this tuition. Depending on which institution you choose, you can spend from a few hundred dollars a year to tens of thousands. Fees, on the other hand, are the much smaller charges that you'll see on your bill; they help fund things like student activities, clubs, athletics, and other non-coursework related events.

For example, John Jay College of Criminal Justice, a liberal arts college within the City University of New York system, charges in-state residents $1,600 per semester in tuition if they are full-time students taking 12 or more credit hours. Tuition for part-time, in-state residents is $135 per credit hour. Foreign students and out-of-state residents can expect to pay $3,275 per credit hour.

Fees for a full-time student (12 or more credit hours) at John Jay are $50.75 per semester. A part-time student (less than 12 credit hours) pays $41.00 per semester. As you can see, fees are much easier on the pocketbook than tuition.

As we mentioned before, community colleges are usually the least expensive choices for education once you leave high school. The U.S. Department of Education found that most community colleges charge under $1,500 per year on average for tuition and fees. They also found plenty of four-year colleges and universities (public institutions, not private) that charge less than $3,000 per year in tuition and fees.

For instance, Sante Fe Community College located in Sante Fe, New Mexico, charges their full-time students $20 per credit hour ($240 for one semester, $480 for the year) if the student lives in the college's district. The maximum they will charge for summer semester tuition is $120. Out-of-district students will pay $26 per credit hour; out-of-state students will pay $48 per credit hour.

Tuition and fees aren't the only costs to consider, of course. Other costs for attending college include:

- books and supplies
- room and board (on- or off-campus)
- transportation costs
- miscellaneous expenses

FINANCIAL AID

Your head is probably reeling from all the math talk. And you are probably wondering how you are going to pay the tab, no matter how inexpensive it might be. That's where financial aid comes in.

There are three kinds of financial aid:

1. Grants and Scholarships—"free" money, as far as you are concerned. You do not pay these gifts back. (More details on these at the end of the chapter.)

2. Loans—You can get loans that are backed by state and federal dollars to finance your education. Don't get them confused with grants or scholarships because you must repay these loans with interest. Fortunately, interest rates on student loans are usually lower than any other kind of loan.

3. Work Study—Your school finds the job, you do the work, and you get the paycheck. You are expected to use the money to help with educational expenses.

Although numbers 1 and 3 can help to offset the costs of higher education, they usually don't give you enough money to pay your way entirely. Most students whose families can't afford to pay for the entire experience rely upon student loans. There are few ways around it—getting an education means spending money. But you don't necessarily have to put *your* money up front. Institutions, the government, and even private funds can help to finance your education. You can get excellent detailed information about different sources of federal education funding by sending away for a copy of the U.S. Department of Education's publication, *The Student Guide.* Write to:

Federal Student Aid Information Center
P.O. Box 84
Washington, DC 20044
or give them a call at:
1-800-4FED-AID

If you want information about financial aid on a state-by-state basis, contact the organizations below. If they can't answer your questions, they'll refer you to someone who can.

Alabama

Executive Director
Commission on Higher Education
100 North Union Street
Montgomery, Alabama 36104-3702
(334) 242-1998
FAX: 242-0268

Alaska

Executive Director
Alaska Commission on Postsecondary
Education
3030 Vintage Boulevard
Juneau, Alaska 99801-7109
(907) 465-2962
FAX: 465-5316

Arizona

Executive Director
Arizona Board of Regents
2020 North Central, Suite 230
Phoenix, Arizona 85004
(602) 229-2500
FAX: 229-2555

Arkansas

Director
Department of Higher Education
114 East Capitol
Little Rock, Arkansas 72201
(501) 324-9300
FAX: 324-9308

California

California Student Aid Commission
P.O. Box 510845
Sacramento, California 94245-0845
(916) 445-0880
FAX: 327-6599

Colorado

Executive Director
Commission on Higher Education
1300 Broadway, 2nd Floor
Denver, Colorado 80203
(303) 866-4034
FAX: 860-9750

Connecticut

Commissioner of Higher Education
Department of Higher Education
61 Woodland Street
Hartford, Connecticut 06105
(203) 566-5766
FAX: 566-7865

Delaware

Executive Director
Delaware Higher Education
Commission
820 French Street, 4th Floor
Wilmington, Delaware 19801
(302) 577-3240
FAX: 577-6765

District of Columbia

Chief, Office of Postsecondary Ed.
Research and Assistance
2100 M. L. King Jr. Avenue, S.E. #401
Washington, D.C. 20020
(202) 727-3685
FAX: 727-2739

Florida

Executive Director
Postsecondary Education Planning
Commission
Florida Education Center
Collins Building
Tallahassee, Florida 32399-0400
(904) 488-7894
FAX: 922-5388

Office of Student Financial Assistance
Room 255, Collins Building
Tallahassee, Florida 32399-0400
(904) 488-1034
FAX: 488-3612

Georgia

Georgia Student Finance Commission
2082 East Exchange Place
Tucker, Georgia 30084
(770) 414-3200
FAX: 414-3163

Hawaii

Hawaii State Postsecondary Education
Commission
2444 Dole Street
Bachman Hall, Room 209
Honolulu, Hawaii 96822
(808) 956-8213
FAX: 956-5156

Idaho

Executive Director for Higher
Education
State Board of Education
P.O. Box 83720
Boise, Idaho 83720-0037
(208) 334-2270
FAX: 334-2632

Illinois

Illinois Student Assistance
Commission
Executive Offices
500 West Monroe Street, 3rd Floor
Springfield, Illinois 62704
(217) 782-6767
 FAX: 524-1858

Indiana

State Student Assistance Commission
of Indiana
150 West Market Street, Suite 500
Indianapolis, Indiana 46204
(317) 232-2350
FAX: 232-3260

Iowa

Iowa College Student Aid Commission
200 Tenth Street, 4th Floor
Des Moines, Iowa 50309
(515) 281-3501
FAX: 242-5996

Kansas

Executive Director, Kansas Board of
Regents
700 SW Harrison, Suite 1410
Topeka, Kansas 66603-3760
(913) 296-3421
FAX: 296-0983

Kentucky

Kentucky Higher Education Assistance
Authority
1050 U.S. 127 South
Frankfort, Kentucky 40601
(502) 564-7990
FAX: 564-7103

Louisiana

Office of Student Financial Assistance,
Louisiana Student Financial Assistance
Commission
P.O. Box 91202
Baton Rouge, Louisiana 70821-9202
(504) 922-1011
FAX: 922-1089

Maine

Financial Authority of Maine, Maine
Education Assistance Division
One Weston Court
State House, Station 119
Augusta, Maine 04333
(207) 287-2183
FAX: 287-2233 or 628-8208

Maryland

Secretary of Higher Education
Maryland Higher Education
Commission
16 Francis Street
Annapolis, Maryland 21401-1781
(410) 974-2971
FAX: 974-3513

Massachusetts

Massachusetts State Scholarship Office
330 Stuart Street
Boston, Massachusetts 02116
(617) 727-9420
FAX: 727-0667

Michigan

Michigan Higher Education Assistance
Authority
P.O. Box 30462
Lansing, Michigan 48909
(517) 373-3394
FAX: 335-5984

Michigan Higher Education Student
Loan Authority
State Department of Education
P.O. Box 30057
Lansing, Michigan 48909
(517) 373-3662
FAX: 335-6699

Minnesota

Executive Director
Higher Education Services Office
400 Capital Square Building
550 Cedar Street
St. Paul, Minnesota 55101
(612) 296-9665
FAX: 297-8880

Mississippi

Commissioner
Board of Trustees of State Institutions
of Higher Learning
3825 Ridgewood Road
Jackson, Mississippi 39211-6453
(601) 982-6611
FAX: 364-2862

Missouri

Commissioner of Higher Education
Coordinating Board for Higher
Education
3515 Amazonas
Jefferson City, Missouri 65109
(314) 751-2361
FAX: 751-6635

Montana

Commissioner of Higher Education
Montana University System
2500 Broadway
Helena, Montana 59620-3101
(406) 444-6570
FAX: 444-1469

Nebraska

Coordinating Commission for Post-
secondary Education
P.O. Box 95005
Lincoln, Nebraska 68509-5005
(402) 471-2847
FAX: 471-2886

Nevada

Nevada Department of Education
700 East 5th Street, Capitol Complex
Carson City, Nevada 89710
(702) 687-5915
FAX: 687-5660

New Hampshire

Executive Director
New Hampshire Postsecondary Educa-
tion Commission
Two Industrial Park Drive
Concord, New Hampshire 03301-8512
(603) 271-2555
FAX: 271-2696

New Jersey

New Jersey Department of Higher
Education
Office of Student Assistance and Information Systems
4 Quakerbridge Plaza, CN 540
Trenton, New Jersey 08625
1-800-792-8670
(609) 584-9618
FAX: 588-2228

New Mexico

Executive Director
Commission on Higher Education
1068 Cerrillos Road
Santa Fe, New Mexico 87501-4295
(505) 827-7383
FAX: 827-7392

New York

The New York State Higher Education
Services Corporation
99 Washington Avenue
Albany, New York 12255
(518) 473-0431
FAX: 474-2839

North Carolina

North Carolina State Education Assistance Authority (NCSEAA)
P.O. Box 2688
Chapel Hill, North Carolina 27515-
2688
(919) 549-8614
FAX: 549-8481

College Foundation, Inc.
P.O. Box 12100
Raleigh, North Carolina 27605
(919) 821-4771
FAX: 821-3139

North Dakota

Chancellor
North Dakota University System
600 East Boulevard Avenue
Bismarck, North Dakota 58505
(701) 328-2962
FAX: 328-2961

Ohio

Chancellor
Ohio Board of Regents
30 East Broad Street, 36th Floor
Columbus, Ohio 43266-0417
(614) 466-0887
FAX: 466-5866

Oklahoma

Chancellor
State Regents for Higher Education
500 Education Building
State Capitol Complex
Oklahoma City, Oklahoma 73105
(405) 524-9100
FAX: 524-9230

Oregon

Oregon State Scholarship Commission
1500 Valley River Drive, Suite 100
Eugene, Oregon 97401
(541) 687-7400
FAX: 687-7419

Pennsylvania

Pennsylvania Higher Education
Assistance Agency
1200 North 7th Street
Harrisburg, Pennsylvania 17102
(717) 257-2850
FAX: 720-3907

Rhode Island

Rhode Island Higher Education
Assistance Authority
560 Jefferson Boulevard
Warwick, Rhode Island 02886
(401) 736-1100
FAX: 732-3541

South Carolina

South Carolina Higher Education
Tuition Grants Commission
P.O. Box 12159
Columbia, South Carolina 29211
(803) 734-1200
FAX: 734-1426

South Dakota

Executive Director
Board of Regents
207 East Capitol Avenue
Pierre, South Dakota 57501-3159
(605) 773-3455
FAX: 773-5320

Department of Education and Cultural
Affairs, Office of the Secretary
700 Governors Drive
Pierre, South Dakota 57501-2291
(605) 773-3134
FAX: 773-6139

Tennessee

Tennessee Student Assistance
Corporation
Parkway Towers, Suite 1950
404 James Robertson Parkway
Nashville, Tennessee 37243-0820
(615) 741-1346
FAX: 741-6101

Texas

Texas Higher Education Coordinating
Board
P.O. Box 12788, Capitol Station
Austin, Texas 78711
(512) 483-6340
FAX: 483-6420

Utah

Commissioner of Higher Education
Utah System of Higher Education
3 Triad Center, Suite 550
Salt Lake City, Utah 84180-1205
(801) 321-7101
FAX: 321-7199

Vermont

Vermont Student Assistance
Corporation
P.O. Box 2000, Champlain Mill
Winooski, Vermont 05404-2601
(802) 655-9602
FAX: 654-3765

Virginia

Director
State Council of Higher Education
101 North 14th Street, 9th Floor
Richmond, Virginia 23219
(804) 225-2600
FAX: 225-2604

Washington

Executive Director
Higher Education Coordinating Board
917 Lakeridge Way, P.O. Box 43430
Olympia, Washington 98504-3430
(360) 753-7800
FAX: 753-7808

West Virginia

Chancellor
State College System of West Virginia
1018 Kanawha Boulevard, East
Charleston, West Virginia 25301
(304) 558-0699
FAX: 558-1011

Chancellor
University of West Virginia System
1018 Kanawha Boulevard, East, Suite
700
Charleston, West Virginia 25301
(304) 558-2736
FAX: 558-3264

Wisconsin

Higher Educational Aids Board
P.O. Box 7885
Madison, Wisconsin 53707
(608) 267-2206
FAX: 267-2808

Wyoming

The Community College Commission
2020 Carey Avenue, 8th Floor
Cheyenne, WY 82002
(307) 777-7763
FAX: 777-6567

Financial aid officers are great people to know; they'll help you sort through your options and complete the necessary paperwork to apply for funding. Show off your investigative skills by doing some searching on your own. Go to your public library and review the reference materials published on the subject of financial aid. The material will be staggering! Be sure to tell the reference librarian what you are trying to accomplish so he or she can point you in the right direction.

More on Grants and Scholarships

As we mentioned before, money from scholarships and grants shouldn't be overlooked, but you can't count on them as the *sole* means of financing your college education. Huge scholarship awards, grants, and the lottery have one thing in common: the odds of winning big money probably aren't in your favor. Then again, someone has to win them, so that's not to say that you shouldn't try. We are saying, however, that you need to have realistic expectations. For one thing, the amount of the award is usually small: from a couple of hundred dollars to *maybe* $1,000-$5,000.

An example of a scholarship in the $1,000-range is the Lt. Gen. Eugene F. Tighe, Jr., USAF Memorial Scholarship. This scholarship is based on academic achievement and is limited to criminal justice majors. You'll need at least a 3.0 GPA to apply, and you must either be in a criminal justice program at the undergraduate or graduate level or be planning to enter a criminal justice program. This $1,000 scholarship is open to both male and female applicants.

For further details, contact:

The Association of Former Intelligence Officers
San Diego Chapter
13785 Quinton Rd.
San Diego, CA 92129

Stellar grades aren't the only criteria used to award scholarships and grants. You may also be eligible for some awards based on other factors: ancestry, gender, financial need, and special relationships (such as children of police officers killed in the line of duty).

An example of a scholarship that takes ancestry into account is one awarded by The National Black Police Association. A $500 scholarship is awarded to one high school senior, male or female, who is African American or who has a minority ancestry. The applicant must have a minimum GPA of 2.5 and must be planning to study criminal justice, law, or a related field. For further information, write to:

The National Black Police Association
3251 Mount Pleasant, NW, 2nd Floor
Washington, DC 20010
(202) 986-2070

Even a background in sports might come in handy. Contact the NCAA at (913) 339-1906 to find out what scholarships and other funding is available for athletes.

There are also scholarships for students who are attending, or are planning to attend, a specific kind of college, university, or trade school. For example, the Law Enforcement Women's Association Criminal Justice Scholarship has a scholarship reserved for students who are community college-bound. This scholarship is for students studying, or planning to study, criminal justice, juvenile justice, corrections, or police science. You must be a resident of North Carolina to apply, and it's open to both female and male applicants who are high school seniors, or college freshmen or sophomores. It's for community college students *only*. To find out about more this scholarship, contact:

North Carolina Department of Community Colleges
200 West Jones Street
Raleigh, NC 27603-1337
(919) 733-7051 x319

Whatever you do, don't waste your money by paying some company to give you a list of available scholarships! Your high school guidance counselor or college financial aid specialist has access to this information and will help free of charge. And the Internet has site after site listing scholarship programs and grants *free* for the searching. One excellent site you should check out is FastWEB, a free database of scholarships and other financial aid information. FastWEB's site address is: *www.studentservices.com/fastweb*.

Other free sites you can find on the web with scholarship and financial aid information are:

Site Name	Site Address
Fundsnet	www.fundsnetservices.com
Scholarship and Fellowship Program Web Pages	www.finaid.org/finaid/awards/award-web.html
Scholarships: On the Net (1100)	www.advocacy-net.com/scholarmks.htm

POLICE CORPS

The U.S. Department of Justice has quite an offer for you if you are willing to make a commitment to policing. If you agree to work in a state or local police force for a minimum of four years, the Police Corps program will contribute funds to cover the following expenses:

- tuition
- fees
- books
- supplies
- transportation
- room and board

They have money for miscellaneous costs as well. You can receive up to $7,500 per academic year, for a total of up to $30,000. This program is designed primarily for students who do not have prior policing experience; those who fall into this category have until 1999 to take advantage of this opportunity. What's in it for the police department who agrees to hire you? They'll get $10,000 for each year of required service that you complete. Give the U.S. Department of Justice Response Center a call at 1-800-421-6770 for specifics, including a detailed listing of participating states and points of contact.

Who:	Don W. Farley
What:	Sheriff
Where:	Rockingham County Sheriff's Office, Virginia
How long:	Over two years

Insider's Advice

First, you must get your foot in the door. By this I mean you should try to get an intern position (paid or unpaid) in the agency of your choice. Not only will you get valuable experience and find out if you really enjoy the work, but those in hiring positions get to evaluate you. I will hire a known quantity much faster than someone that looks good on an application. One thing that I take into consideration is the all-important "first impression." I look for someone that will look me in the eyes and extend a firm and warm handshake. Proper dress is very important. I don't care if you are interviewing for the animal warden or maintenance position, you should come to the interview looking your Sunday best.

Insider's Take on the Future

Getting a college degree can never hurt you. It shows that you have goals and can finish what you start. On the other hand, I know degree-holding people that can't tie their shoes. It takes a tremendous amount of common sense and the ability to work with people from all levels of society to be an effective law enforcement officer.

CHAPTER | 5

This chapter explores military service as a step toward a law enforcement career. You'll find out why veterans are given a hiring preference in most law enforcement agencies, why employers think men and women with military training make great cops and agents, and how Uncle Sam will help pay for the college education you'll need. You'll also get a look at what the military selection process and training is like; details on what to expect from the Army, Navy, Air Force, and Marines; and advice on how to decide which branch of the military is right for you.

THE MILITARY OPTION

With few exceptions, law enforcement agencies don't hire anyone who hasn't cut his or her 21st birthday cake. If all you've ever dreamed about was becoming a law enforcement officer, but you aren't old enough, this is bound to be frustrating! If this describes your situation, it's best to set aside your frustration and put this time to good use.

The minimum age for employment is set at 21 by law enforcement agencies for many reasons, the least of which being that 21 is the age at which most states consider a person to have reached legal adulthood. It's also because employers want applicants who are mature, have life experience, and have proven to be responsible adults. Sergeant Julie O'Brien, a supervisor for the Austin Police Department and an Army veteran says:

Lack of life experience is the hardest obstacle to overcome. I think it's harder to do the job when you don't have much life experience. What you are likely to see in law enforcement can be overwhelming enough if you already have life experience; it can be much harder to deal with if you are coming at the situation without it. You can get life experience in the military.

No, we're not getting a kick-back from Uncle Sam for saying this. The military *is* one place where you can develop all the desirable qualities and get the life experience to put you ahead of your competition when you're old enough to apply for civilian law enforcement jobs.

THE ADVANTAGE

There's another benefit to considering military service: veteran's preference points. Veterans of military service are generally given preference points by most law enforcement agencies at local, state, and federal levels. Congress enacted laws long ago to make sure that those who serve their country aren't denied civilian jobs after they are discharged from the service. This means that many agencies will automatically add points to the scores of veterans who apply to their agencies. At the federal level, veterans can receive anywhere from 5 to 10 preference points, depending on the circumstances surrounding their military career.

If police work is your ultimate goal, you should know that President Clinton has made hiring military veterans very attractive to police departments. As part of his strategy to put more cops on the street, he recently supported a federal grant that pays participating police departments $10,000 for every veteran they hire (as long as the veteran held a job in the military that meets certain requirements). Before departments are paid, however, that veteran has to pass all police officer training and licensing requirements.

That's not the only advantage. Additionally, law enforcement managers seem to prefer having veterans in their ranks. Sergeant O'Brien explains:

I like to have former military personnel on my shift because they know the system. The structures of police departments are always going to be paramilitary so prior military personnel have an advantage because they are familiar with rank structure. They also react well in tactical situations—they follow orders quickly and without question.

THE ENLISTED ROUTE

If you decide that going straight into the military after high school is the best option for you while you wait for that all-important birthday, your next decision will be which branch of the service to choose. For instance, if you don't like to swim and hate the beach, you might want to walk past the Navy recruiter's booth. Take your time and research your options carefully. After all, this is one decision you will have to live with for several years, depending on the enlistment program you choose.

The Beginning

Begin your search for the right branch of the armed services with a quick glance in your phone book's yellow pages under "Recruiting." This will give you the phone numbers and addresses of the nearest military recruiting offices, or you can look in the government blue pages for each of the individual branches. Or, feel free to use Uncle Sam's quarter to call these toll-free numbers:

U.S. Army	1-800-USA-ARMY
U.S. Air Force	1-800-423-USAF
U.S. Navy	1-800-USA-NAVY
U.S. Marines	1-800-MARINES
U.S. Coast Guard	1-800-424-8883

Don't rush to narrow your options. If you're thinking of spending a few years in the military, visiting a recruiter from each of the four branches—Army, Navy, Air Force, and Marines—can't hurt. There are many similarities, but the subtle differences in what each branch of service has to offer could make a lot of difference in the long run.

Basic Requirements

There are certain requirements you will have to meet in order to enlist in any branch of the military. You must:

- be between 17 and 34 years of age, and have a parent or guardian's permission if you are under 18
- be a U.S. citizen
- have a high school diploma or GED
- be drug-free
- have a clean arrest record

> ### Documents You'll Need
>
> You'll have to present certain documents not only to your recruiter when you first start the enlistment process, but also at various points along the way. Have the following documentation available to save yourself a lot of last minute panic and hassle:
>
> - a birth certificate or other proof of citizenship and date of birth
> - a valid social security card or two other pieces of social security identification
> - a high school diploma or GED certificate
> - a letter or transcript documenting your midterm graduation from high school, if applicable
> - a college transcript, if applicable, showing credits earned
> - a parental or guardian consent form if you are under 18 years old
> - a doctor's letter if you have, or have a history of, special medical condition(s)
> - a marriage certificate, if applicable
> - divorce papers, if applicable

Working with Your Recruiter

The recruiter is there to help you *and* to get your signature on the dotted line. In speaking with him or her, be sure to ask detailed questions and make certain you understand exactly what will be required of you. Tony Gifford, a military police officer in the Army, discovered that sometimes people aren't aware of what military assignments are truly like:

> People coming into the Army's MP are not aware that you do not just do law enforcement. You spend a lot of time in foreign countries keeping the peace, or whatever the Army wants you to do. Also, a lot of time is spent in the field training for combat. I don't mind it, but I was not aware of that until I got into the Army.

Make sure the recruiter understands that you want all promises to be in writing on your service contract before you'll consider signing. This will clear up any lingering confusion and will obligate the service to keep their promises. Don't be afraid to bring along a parent or a trusted friend to help you ask questions. A professional military recruiter won't mind the extra set of eyes and ears.

Ask about the service and its benefits: salaries, fringe benefits, postings, and educational opportunities, including financial aid for college. (See the table on the next page for the basic salaries of various grades of enlisted personnel in all the service branches.) The recruiter will also ask about your: education, physical and mental health, goals, interests, hobbies, and life experience. This will be the perfect time to talk about your desire to be a law enforcement agent!

You'll also be given a brief test designed to give the recruiter an idea of how well you'll perform on the Armed Services Vocational Aptitude Battery (ASVAB). This pre-test covers math and vocabulary. Although the ASVAB has ten different subtests, it's the math and verbal portions that determine whether or not you pass. The other sections are designed to determine what your aptitudes are for different jobs.

You and your recruiter should also discuss the kinds of jobs available to you in the military. But before that discussion can take place, you'll have to be tested to see if you can enlist and what specialties you qualify for. That's where your trip to the Military Entrance Processing Station comes in.

Military Entrance Processing Station (MEPS)

Your recruiter will schedule you for a trip to a MEPS in your area (there's one in nearly every state) for a day of written and physical testing. You'll travel as a guest of Uncle Sam by plane, train, bus, or car, depending on how far away you live from the nearest facility. MEPS schedules may vary a little from area to area, but they all operate five days per week and are open some Saturdays. If for any reason you're asked to stay overnight for testing, then the military will pick up the bill for your hotel room and meals.

The MEPS is where every applicant for each branch of the military begins the enlistment process, so even if the Marine Corps is your future employer, you can expect to see staff wearing Navy blue, Army green, or Air Force blue. When you enter the MEPS, you'll check in at the control desk, and then be sent to the liaison office for your chosen branch of service.

Your MEPS Day at a Glance

During your day at MEPS you'll go through three phases:

- ◆ mental (aptitude) testing
- ◆ medical exam
- ◆ administrative procedures

1997 military base pay chart

Grade	<2	2	3	4	6	8	10	12	14	16	18	20	22	24	26
Years of Service															
Commissioned officers															
O-10	7360.20	7619.10	7619.10	7619.10	7619.10	7911.60	7911.60	8349.90	8349.90	8947.20	8947.20	9546.30	9546.30	9546.30	10140.90
O-9	6522.90	6693.90	6858.70	6836.70	6835.70	7010.60	7010.40	7202.00	7202.00	7911.60	7911.60	8349.90	8349.90	8349.90	8947.20
O-8	5908.20	6085.50	6229.80	6229.80	6229.80	6693.90	6692.90	7010.40	7010.40	7302.00	7619.10	7911.60	8106.60	8106.60	8106.60
O-7	4909.20	5243.10	5243.10	5243.10	5478.30	5478.30	5795.70	6085.50	6095.50	6693.90	7154.40	7302.00	7154.40	7154.40	7154.40
O-6	3638.40	3997.50	4259.70	4259.70	4259.70	4259.70	4259.70	4259.70	4404.60	5100.90	5361.30	5478.30	5795.70	5991.60	6285.60
O-5	2910.30	3417.00	3653.40	3653.40	3653.40	3653.50	3763.50	3966.60	4232.40	4549.20	4809.60	4955.70	5128.80	5128.80	5128.80
O-4	2452.80	2987.10	3186.30	3186.30	3186.30	3245.40	3619.80	3823.20	3997.50	4173.30	4287.90	4287.90	4287.90	4287.90	4287.90
O-3	2279.40	2548.50	2724.90	3014.70	3159.00	3272.10	3449.40	3619.80	3708.60	3708.60	3708.60	3708.60	3708.60	3708.60	3708.60
O-2	1987.80	2178.80	2608.20	2695.80	2751.60	2751.60	2751.60	2751.60	2751.60	2751.60	2751.60	2751.60	2751.60	2751.60	2751.60
O-1	1725.90	1796.10	2170.80	2170.80	2170.80	2170.80	2170.80	2170.80	2170.80	2170.80	2170.80	2170.80	2170.80	2170.80	2170.80
Officers with more than 4 years active duty as enlisted or warrant officer															
O-3E	0.00	0.00	0.00	3014.70	3159.00	3272.10	3449.40	3619.80	3763.50	3763.50	3763.50	3763.50	3763.50	3763.50	3763.50
O-2E	0.00	0.00	0.00	2695.80	2751.60	2838.90	2987.10	3101.40	3186.30	3186.30	3186.30	3186.30	3186.30	3186.30	3186.30
O-1E	0.00	0.00	0.00	2170.80	2319.30	2404.50	2491.80	2578.20	2695.80	2695.80	2695.80	2695.80	2695.80	2695.80	2695.80
Warrant officers															
W-5	0.00	0.00	0.00	0.00	0.00	0.00	0.00	0.00	0.00	0.00	0.00	3963.60	4113.60	4232.70	4410.90
W-4	2322.30	2491.80	2491.80	2548.50	2664.60	2781.90	2898.60	3101.40	3245.40	3359.40	3449.40	3560.70	3679.80	3794.40	3966.60
W-3	2110.80	2289.60	2289.60	2319.30	2346.30	2517.90	2664.60	2751.60	2838.90	2923.80	3014.70	3132.30	3245.40	3245.40	3359.40
W-2	1848.60	2000.10	2000.10	2058.30	2170.80	2289.60	2376.60	2463.60	2548.50	2638.20	2724.90	2810.40	2923.80	2923.80	2923.80
W-1	1540.20	1765.80	1765.80	1913.40	2000.10	2085.90	2170.80	2260.20	2346.30	2433.60	2517.90	2608.20	2608.20	2608.20	2608.20
Enlisted members															
E-9	0.00	0.00	0.00	0.00	0.00	0.00	2701.80	2762.40	2824.80	2889.90	2954.70	3011.70	3169.80	3293.40	3478.50
E-8	0.00	0.00	0.00	0.00	0.00	2265.60	2330.70	2391.90	2454.00	2519.10	2578.40	2639.70	2794.80	2919.30	3106.50
E-7	1581.90	1707.90	1770.60	1833.00	1895.40	1955.70	2018.40	2081.40	2175.30	2237.10	2298.90	2329.20	2485.50	2609.10	2794.80
E-6	1360.80	1483.50	1545.00	1610.70	1671.30	1731.30	1794.90	1887.30	1946.70	2009.40	2040.00	2040.00	2040.00	2040.00	2040.00
E-5	1194.30	1299.90	1362.90	1422.30	1515.90	1577.70	1639.80	1700.40	1731.30	1731.30	1731.30	1731.30	1731.30	1731.30	1731.30
E-4	1113.60	1176.30	1245.60	1341.90	1394.70	1394.70	1394.70	1394.70	1394.70	1394.70	1394.70	1394.70	1394.70	1394.70	1394.70
E-3	1049.70	1107.00	1151.10	1196.70	1196.70	1196.70	1196.70	1196.70	1196.70	1196.70	1196.70	1196.70	1196.70	1196.70	1196.70
E-2	1010.10	1010.10	1010.10	1010.10	1010.10	1010.10	1010.10	1010.10	1010.10	1010.10	1010.10	1010.10	1010.10	1010.10	1010.10
E-1>4	900.90	900.90	900.90	900.90	900.90	900.90	900.90	900.90	900.90	900.90	900.90	900.90	900.90	900.90	900.90
E-1 with less than 4 months—$833.40															

Note: Basic pay is limited to $9016.80 per month. Figures for 0-10 in the chart show what pay would be without the cap.

Your schedule may vary somewhat from the one outlined here, depending on how much of the process you have completed in advance. Some applicants, for example, may have already taken the ASVAB at a Mobile Examining Team (MET) site near their hometown recruiting station.

Mental (Aptitude) Testing

Your day at the MEPS will most likely begin with the ASVAB, if you haven't already taken it. Don't underestimate the impact the ASVAB will have on your entry into the military. Results of the ASVAB test and the physical and mental exam you receive during the entrance process are used to determine whether or not you can join the branch of the military you prefer, and which training programs you are qualified to enter. So make sure you are rested and ready—keep the partying to a minimum the night before you leave for the MEPS. (See LearningExpress' *Armed Services Vocational Aptitude Battery [ASVAB]* study guide for help in preparing for this test.)

Some MEPS are now conducting ASVAB testing on computer. The computer version of the test takes one hour and forty minutes to complete, as opposed to over three hours for the paper-and-pencil version. The computer ASVAB still consists of ten subtests, but it works differently than the paper version. The computer will display the first question, and, if you get this question right, it gives you another question on the same subject—but this question is a bit harder than the first one. The questions get harder as you progress, and, after you answer a certain number correctly, the computer skips to the next subtest. For example, you could get eight questions right and then the computer might go to the next subtest instead of requiring you to answer all 25 questions in that one subtest.

Most MEPS do not have enough computers to test everyone. If you notice that some applicants are taken to a room with computer testing and the others are required to take the ASVAB with pen and paper, don't worry. Either way, the information and skills you need remain the same, and your evaluation won't be affected.

Medical Exam

Next on the list in your busy day at the MEPS is the medical exam. All of the doctors you will see here are civilians. You'll see them at least three times during the day. During the first visit, you and the medical staff will thoroughly review your medical prescreening form, your medical history form, and all of the medical records you've been told by your recruiter to bring along. This meeting will be one-on-one.

After this meeting, you'll move on to the examining room. You'll strip down to your underwear and perform a series of about 20 exercises that will let the medical staff see how your limbs and joints work. You may be with a group of other applicants of the same sex during this examination, or you may be alone with the doctor.

During your third meeting with the doctor you will receive a routine physical. Among the procedures you can expect are:

- blood pressure evaluation
- pulse rate evaluation
- heart and lung check
- evaluation of blood and urine samples
- eye exam
- hearing exam
- height-proportional-to-weight check
- chest X-ray
- HIV testing

Female applicants will be given a pelvic/rectal examination. Another woman will be present during this procedure, but otherwise this exam will be conducted in private.

After these checks, you'll find out whether your physical condition passes muster. If the medical staff uncovers a problem that will keep you from joining the service, they will discuss the matter with you. In some cases the doctor may tell you that you are being disqualified at the moment, but that you can come back at a later date to try again. For example, if you are overweight, you could lose a few pounds and then come back to the MEPS for another try.

If the doctor wants to have a medical specialist examine you for some reason, you may have to stay overnight, or the doctor may schedule an appointment for a later date (at the military's expense, of course). Unless you need to see a specialist, the medical exam should take no more than three hours.

The Paper Chase

The rest of your day will be taken up with administrative concerns. First you'll meet with a guidance counselor for your branch of the service. He or she will take the results of your physical, your ASVAB scores, and all the other information you have provided and enter it into a computer system. The computer will show which military jobs are best suited to you. Then you can begin asking questions about your career options. Before you leave the room you'll know:

- which jobs you are qualified for
- which jobs suit your personality, abilities, and interests
- which jobs are available
- when the required training is available

You'll also be able to decide whether you prefer to enter the military on this very day or to enlist under the Delayed Entry Program. Some applicants raise their right hand during swearing-in ceremonies at the end of the processing day, while others prefer to go home and decide what they want to do.

Whichever way you go, it's critical that you ask as many questions as possible during this visit with the counselor. Take your time, and be sure you know what you want before you go any further in the process. Be aware, though, that the seats in the popular training programs go fast. The earlier you make your decision, the more likely you'll get what you really want.

Enlistment Durations by Branch

Branch of Service	Terms of Enlistment
Army	2, 4, or 6 years
Navy	3, 4, 5, or 6 years
Air Force	4 or 6 years
Marines	3, 4, or 5 years

Delayed Entry Programs

Delayed Entry Programs allow you to enlist with your chosen branch of the military and report for duty up to 365 days later. This is a popular program for students who are still in high school or for those who have other obligations that prevent them from leaving for basic training right away.

Basic Training

Everything you've done so far has been leading up to this moment: the day you leave for Basic Training. You'll report back to the MEPS to prepare for Basic Training. If you've been in the Delayed Entry Program, you'll get a last minute mini-physical to make sure your condition is still up to par. You'll also be asked about any changes that might affect your eligibility since the last time you were at the MEPS. If you've been arrested or had any medical problems, now is the time to speak up.

Your orders and records will be completed at the MEPS, and then you're on your way to Basic, by plane, bus, or car (again, at the military's expense). Where you train will depend on the branch of service. The Air Force and Navy have only one training facility each. The Marines have two, and the Army has several, because where the Army sends you will depend on which specialized training you selected at the MEPS.

Basic Training (by Branch)

Branch	Location of Basic Training Facility	Length of Training
Army	Fort Benning, GA; Fort Knox, KT; Fort Sill, OK; Fort Bliss, TX; Fort Leonard Wood, MI; or Fort McClellan, AL	8 weeks
Navy	Recruit Training Command, Great Lakes, IL	8 weeks and 3 days
Air Force	Lackland Air Force Base, TX	6 weeks
Marine Corps	Parris Island, SC,* or San Diego, CA	Women: 12 weeks; Men: 11 weeks, plus 4 weeks of combat training

*All women Marines attend Basic at Parris Island.

The First Few Days

No matter which branch of service you join, the first few days of Basic are pretty much the same. You'll spend time at an intake facility, where you'll be assigned to a basic training unit and undergo a quick-paced introduction to your branch of service. Your days will include:

+ orientation briefings
+ uniform distribution
+ records processing
+ I.D. card preparation

- barracks upkeep training
- drill and ceremony instruction
- physical training (PT)

You'll be assigned to a group of recruits ranging from 35 to 80 people. The Navy calls these training groups "companies," the Army and Marine Corps call them "platoons," and the Air Force calls them "flights." And let's not forget your "supervisor" for these early days of your military career—the drill instructor. This is the person who greets you early in the morning, is your primary instructor throughout the day, and tucks you in at night—though not as tenderly as you might hope.

The Following Weeks

From the intake facility, you'll go to your Basic Training site. You can expect your training day to start around 5 a.m. and officially end around 9 p.m. Most Saturdays and Sundays are light training days. You won't have much free time, and your ability to travel away from your unit on weekends will be very limited, if you get this privilege at all. In most cases you will not be eligible to take leave (vacation time) until after Basic Training, although exceptions may be made in the case of a family emergency.

The subjects you learn in Basic Training include:

- military courtesy
- military regulations
- military rules of conduct
- hygiene and sanitation
- organization and mission
- handling and care of weapons
- tactics and training related specifically to your service

While you are in Basic Training you can expect plenty of physical training, all the better to prepare you for law enforcement training down the road. Physical fitness is critical for trainees ("Trainee" is your new first name), and your drill instructor will keep tabs on your progress throughout Basic Training by giving you periodical tests. Your best bet is to start a running and weight-lifting program *the instant* you make your decision to join the military. Recruits in all branches of the service run mile after mile, perform hundreds of sit-ups and push-ups, and become closely acquainted with obstacle courses. These courses differ in appearance from facility to facility, but they all require the same things: plenty of upper body strength and overall endurance, as well as the will to succeed.

Lifetime Memories

Basic Training, no matter which branch of the service you choose, is a time in your life that you will never forget. No one is promising you it will be pleasant, but during this time you'll forge friendships you'll keep for the rest of your life. Years later, you'll laugh with other soldiers, sailors, marines, and airmen about the late nights you spent spit-polishing boots by the light of a flashlight after lights out, or the push-ups you gave your drill sergeant when the buttons on your shirt didn't line up with the button and zipper on your pants. At graduation, your friends and family will notice the changes in you. Your pride in your accomplishments will be obvious, and well deserved. You'll be ready for the challenge of serving your country as you prepare to enter your specialized training course.

The Occupational Specialty for You

No one expects you to go into the military police field just because you want a career in law enforcement. Your future law enforcement employers won't hold it against you, according to Sergeant O'Brien:

> My first order of preference for people I want on my shift is prior
> military experience, regardless of the occupational skills they learned
> in the military.

The military offers training in many areas that will be useful in a civilian law enforcement career. All branches of the military basically offer the same career fields, although they are often called by different names. There are obvious exceptions; you won't see M1 Armor Crewman listed in the Navy because they don't tend to drive armored tanks around their battleships. On the following page is a list of careers that should make your application stand out when you move on to your law enforcement career. Details are available from your recruiter, though they shouldn't vary much from branch to branch. We're using Army titles and Army requirements as examples on this list.

Requirements for Selected Military Occupational Specialities

Military Occupational Speciality	Physical Demands	Minimum ASVAB Composite Score	Other Requirements
Infantryman*	very heavy	CO 90	red/green color discrimination, vision correctable to 20/20 in one eye and 20/100 in the other
PATRIOT Missile Crewmember	moderately heavy	OF 100	red/green color discrimination, SECRET security clearance
Psychological Operations Specialist	medium	ST 105	normal color vision, SECRET security clearance, minimum score on language test
Broadcast Journalist	light	GT 110	ability to type 20 WPM, completion of at least 2 years of high school English, driver's license
Ammunition Specialist	very heavy	ST 100	normal color vision, CONFIDENTIAL security clearance, not allergic to explosive components, not claustrophobic
Executive Administrative Assistant	not applicable	ST 105	SECRET security clearance, ability to type 35 WPM, minimum score on English test
Legal Specialist	light	CL 110	ability to type 35 WPM, no civil convictions
Finance Specialist	light	CL 95	no record of dishonesty or moral turpitude
Watercraft Operator	very heavy	MM 100	normal color vision, vision correctable to 20/20 in one eye and 20/40 in the other, prior training
Medical Specialist	moderately heavy	ST 95	normal color vision
Behavioral Science Specialist	light	ST 105	—
Military Police	moderately heavy	ST 95	red/green color discrimination, minimum height 5' 8" for males, 5' 4" for females, CONFIDENTIAL security clearance, driver's license, no record of civilian convictions
Intelligence Analyst	medium	ST 105	normal color vision, TOP SECRET security clearance, no record, certain restrictions on foreign ties

* Specialties not open to women.

Composite Score key: OF = Operations and Food Handling; ST = Skilled Technician; GT = General Technical; CL = Clerical; MM = Mechanical Maintenance; CO = Combat.

DOES THIS MEAN COLLEGE IS OUT OF THE PICTURE?

Certainly not! Nothing's changed. You'll *still* be better off with a college degree if you want to get ahead of your competition. Joining the military right out of high school doesn't mean that you've blown your chance to get your college education, or to get enough college hours to reach the minimum requirement for your dream job. On the contrary, the military makes education programs available while you are on active duty or after you finish your military obligation. Air Force Senior Airman Julius Carl Mitchell earned his degree while on active duty. He is assigned to the Security Force (formerly the Security Police) and recently completed his Associate Degree in Criminal Justice through the Community College of the Air Force. Airman Mitchell says it would have been easier to attend his college classes had he gone into a specialty other than the Security Force, but he completed his degree nonetheless:

> It all depended on where I was stationed at the time. While I was in Korea it was easy. The problem is, law enforcement is a 24-hour organization. It's not hard if you are part of another organization in the Air Force, but since we don't necessarily work 9-to-5, it can be hard to get to class.

There's no reason to think the military will keep you from going after that much-needed diploma. What's more, your future employers may well be impressed with the way you spent your time waiting to become "of age" for a civilian law enforcement career. Sergeant O'Brien says:

> My advice is join the military or get your college education. If you join the military, there's no reason why you can't get your education at the same time. It's a fact that you can communicate better if you are college-educated, and you will most likely need the college hours anyway. I think the military is a good source of life experience, but don't waste your time while you're in there. In a three-year stint you can easily get a two-year degree.

Of course there are other ways to get the military advantage and college credits besides joining the military outright.

U.S. MILITARY ACADEMIES

The decision to attend a military academy doesn't fall into the last minute category! Hopefully, you're reading this paragraph early on in your high school career. You'll need excellent grades and strong recommendations from your high school, not to mention from your state representative, to get into one of these institutions. The competition for admission is fierce because of the prestige and quality of the education. And free tuition in return for your commitment to serve after graduation is certainly a selling point. "Prepare early" is the key phrase here. High school counselors have the information you need to formulate a strategy.

Except for the Marine Corps, each branch of the armed services has an academy. Upon graduation from their institution, you'll receive a bachelor's degree and a commission in the military. The academies are:

- **U.S. Military Academy**, located in West Point, New York
- **U.S. Naval Academy**, located in Annapolis, Maryland
- **U.S. Air Force Academy**, located in Colorado Springs, Colorado

There are two other academy options: the U.S. Coast Guard Academy, located in New London, Connecticut; and the U.S. Merchant Marine Academy, located in Kings Point, New York. They offer the same incentives as the military academies in that they pay your tuition in return for your service in the Coast Guard or Merchant Marines.

RESERVE OFFICERS TRAINING CORPS (ROTC) PROGRAMS

Another way to combine military service and higher education is to enroll in an ROTC program in college. The Navy, Marines, Army, and Air Force all offer ROTC, a college elective that you take along with your regular course work. The best deal is, of course, the ROTC scholarship programs.

Captain Rhonda Lovko, who is currently assigned to the Military Science Department at Santa Clara University in California, has this advice for high school seniors and recent graduates interested in ROTC:

> If you haven't gotten a scholarship by the time you are a senior in high school, it's too late for the first year of college. If you feel you are interested at all in ROTC, then go ahead and try it out for the first year or two. It's just a course, and if you don't like it you aren't under any obligation. You can apply for scholarships once you get past your freshman year.

ROTC scholarship programs will pay most of your tuition, fees, and textbook costs. They'll also give you a monthly allowance while you are in school. In return, you commit to summer training while you are in school, and to serve as an officer in that branch of the service after earning your bachelor's degree. Don't lose sight of one very important factor when you consider this option—payback. In return for the financial support, you will owe service to the branch that gave you the money. Captain Lovko sums it up:

> The hardest part for students to realize is that after you've been given money by the ROTC for your education, the services are going to want something back. You are going to have to go on active duty for at least four years after graduation in return for that money.

All of the ROTC branches have eligibility requirements for you to meet before they'll give you an ROTC scholarship. The Army requires that:

- you must be a U.S. citizen at least 17 years old by October 1, 1998 and under 23 on June 30, 1998. You can't be older than 27 by June 30 of the year you'll graduate from college. If you have prior active-duty military service, you may get an extension of the age requirement: one year extension for every one year of prior service. However, they'll only waive three years total.
- you must have a minimum SAT score of 920 points or an ACT composite score of 19.

The above listed requirements are the primary ones, but the Army does have others for their ROTC scholarships.

A scholarship student can receive an additional $1,500 per year. Non-scholarship students can get that $1,500 per year if they sign a contract with the Army in the last two years of school. After you get your degree and meet the commissioning requirements, you'll join the active Army as a Second Lieutenant earning approximately $26,000 per year in pay and allowances.

If you called the Air Force ROTC at the college of your choice and asked about their program, they'd tell you that their scholarships range in length from two to four years. The Air Force will pay full or partial tuition, give you an allowance for textbooks, and pay most of your fees. Once your scholarship begins, you'll get an additional $150 per month to help with expenses.

To be eligible for an ROTC scholarship with the Air Force, you must be under 27 years of age by June 30 of the year that you receive your commission, unless you are a prior service applicant. You also must pass the Air Force's Physical Fitness Test (PFT), which includes a 1.5 mile run, and then an Air Force medical exam. You must also pass the Air Force Officer Qualifying Test (AFOQT).

The Navy relies on their NRTOC programs for the majority of their Navy and Marine Corps officers. Unlike the Army and Air Force programs, when the NROTC awards you a scholarship, they pay 100% of your tuition, books, and fees no matter where you go to school—public or private. (As in all the ROTC scholarship programs, you'll pay your own room and board.) You'll also get a $150 per month allowance during the school year. Plus, you'll be paid for attending 30 days of active-duty training each summer. After graduation from an NROTC scholarship program, you'll wear ensign bars in either the Naval Reserve or second lieutenant bars in the Marine Corps Reserve.

Remember, if you haven't applied for ROTC scholarships in high school or your grades aren't high enough to win one during your senior year, most of the programs will consider you for a scholarship once you've completed a semester or two of college. Ask your ROTC representative for all the details before you make your decision.

In the chapter three list of colleges and universities offering criminal justice programs, there are ROTC programs listed as well. When you have a good idea of where you'd like to go to school, call the phone numbers you see with each listing and ask about the the ROTC program at that institution. You can also call 1-800-USA-ROTC for additional details and phone numbers.

Captain Lovko, who's also a 1991 graduate of Christopher Newport College's Army ROTC program, has a few thoughts to pass on to women who are interested in ROTC (advice that will serve *both* sexes well):

> I've never felt that this program was any more of a challenge simply because I am female. Don't let *anybody* tell you that you can't do it. It can be a little more challenging as far as physical fitness goes. You have to be in good enough shape to pass the physical testing and you have to meet height and weight requirements. It isn't that hard, but you have to do more than sit on the couch and watch TV to get ready.

THE MONTGOMERY GI BILL

Recruiters rely heavily on this program to entice recruits who are looking for a way to help finance their higher education. You can get up to 36 months of educational benefits through the MGIB for use after you leave the military. You can use the money to get degrees, certificates, correspondence course credits, and vocational flight training. Although you might get quite a different impression from a recruiter, participation in this program does not necessarily mean you'll be able to attend the college of your choice for "free" after your military obligation is over. Like all contracts, read the fine print carefully.

If you decide to participate in this program, you'll be expected to contribute $100 per month for first 12 months of service. This money is not refundable under *any* circumstances and you aren't allowed to withdraw from the program once you commit to it. You'll have up to 10 years to use the education benefit after you leave the military.

Be aware, too, that most colleges and universities have financial aid personnel who are trained specifically to handle military education programs and benefits. Get the full details from your local recruiter, or use one of the Internet search engines (like Yahoo! or Excite) to search the World Wide Web. Use the key words "Montgomery GI Bill." You'll find many informative articles (pro and con), charts, and detailed payment projection information.

NATIONAL GUARD AND RESERVES

Enlisting full-time in the armed services might not be for everyone. The National Guard and Reserve programs offer a good alternative. You'll give up one weekend a month plus 14 days for annual training, and you'll receive the same training and schooling as your active-duty counterparts. These programs can help with college costs and with supplementing your income while you go to school.

All branches of the reserves have made changes to their programs in the past several years to make enlistment more appealing. The benefits have been upgraded and new education incentives have been added. For more information, call:

U.S. Army Reserve	1-800-USA-ARMY
U.S. Navy Reserve	1-800-USA-USNR
U.S. Air Force Reserve	1-800-257-1212
U.S. Army National Guard	1-800-638-7600

Who:	Julius Carl Mitchell
What:	Senior Airman
Where:	Randolph Air Force Base in San Antonio, Texas
How long:	Over eight years in Air Force law enforcement
Degree:	Six weeks of law enforcement academy; four weeks of air base defense; over a year of on-the-job training

Insider's Advice

I wanted to work in law enforcement. When I first got into the Air Force there were two different sides of house, so to speak—security and law enforcement. The security side guarded planes and things like that. On the law enforcement side you got to deal more with people, work investigations—things I wanted to do. I love meeting different kinds of people. I like being there to provide assistance for people that need it.

In a typical day, we have to come in an hour early for each shift. If we're scheduled to work eight-hour shifts, then we really end up putting in nine hours. If we're working 12-hour shifts, which we've been doing a lot lately because we have [personnel] shortages, then we actually put in 13 hours. My current duties are to check equipment in and out: weapons, mace, radios, flashlights.

The first thing we do when we get to work is have Guard Mount, which is like roll call for civilian police officers. The day before you come into work they put a roster out that tells you what kind of duty you will have the next day. The roster isn't official until Guard Mount because if someone gets sick, you might have to take over their assignment if it has a higher priority than yours. If you are assigned to work the gate, then your duties include waving vehicles through the gate (if they have the proper decals), giving people directions if they are new to the base, and just acting as ambassadors for the Air Force.

Insider's Take on the Future

Well, right now might not be a good time to go into the Security Force. They are changing the job duties pretty much. The emphasis will be on air base security and not so much on law enforcement. I'd say don't do it right now because you'll be the Air Force's infantry. But it is a good starting point if you want to get your foot in the door. You'll get good training!

CHAPTER | 6

This chapter gives you detailed advice from recruiting experts on how to put together everything you've learned in order to successfuly market your skills and experience to future employers. You'll learn the secrets behind the law enforcement hiring process, how to earn the respect and admiration of background investigators, and how to survive intimidating oral interviews.

PUTTING IT ALL TOGETHER

G etting the job of your dreams in law enforcement is not something you want to leave to luck. Having a game plan is vital to achieving your goal. This chapter is devoted to helping you come up with a blueprint for success. Whether you are young and have relatively little life experience, or you've been around a while and have more than you'd like to think about, we've got a strategy for how you can prepare for your career in law enforcement.

We polled law enforcement recruiters and managers across the nation about their experiences with both top-notch applicants and ones who didn't quite make the cut, and then boiled their experiences down to a few basic suggestions.

Education

Here it is again! The importance of education can't be emphasized enough. Most of the recruiters we talked to were partial to hiring applicants with college degrees, both because law enforcement hiring trends indicate the need, and because they thought college graduates make better officers and agents. Of course, all agencies want applicants with common sense and good judgment. Unfortunately, no college or university offers a course in either. Speaking of classwork, our experts mentioned that they'll be looking not only at whether or not you have a degree, but *how* you got it. Keep in mind that someday you might be telling a background investigator why you never attended classes and got such poor grades, or you might be watching them nod approvingly over how well you juggled classwork and your part-time job. Investigators will also want to know how you felt and what you learned from the college experience. So, take your grandmother's advice: "Anything worth doing is worth doing well."

Employment

A stable job history is also very important, according to those we polled. Even the part-time job you held in high school at the local Sack 'N Wag will matter. Background investigators will be calling your past employers to find out how you handled your responsibilities. (If you are just starting out in the work force, keep this in mind as you choose your place of employment.) They'll ask if you got to work on time, how you performed your duties, and how well you got along with customers, coworkers, and supervisors. Your work history is one of the scales they will use to measure your level of maturity. If you come up short, you may well hear that phrase: "Why don't you come back and re-apply when you can show us that you are more mature and responsible. . . ."

But suppose you've been in the work force long enough to have a list of previous employers. You can't change the past, so be ready to explain how you handled yourself, why you made the decisions you did, and what you've learned from the experience. Don't be surprised if they ask you what you'd do differently if you had it all to do over. As for the job you hold now, get to work on time, take pride in your work, and hone those communication skills with coworkers and clients/customers!

Finances

The professionals we talked to all agreed that how you handle your financial affairs says a lot about how you handle responsibility. Some told us that they flatly refuse to consider applicants who have excessive amounts of debt or who have a history of financial irresponsibility (i.e., hot checks, failure to pay bills in a timely manner, etc.). Others said that although they may not disqualify applicants for shaky finances, they can guarantee that these applicants will spend a lot of their oral interview explaining their past financial decisions.

If you find yourself in this predicament, your future employer will want to know what you are doing to correct the problem and if you are taking responsibility for your actions. You'll be better off if you go into your interview with solutions for your problems. It's much better to say "As you can see by my recent credit report, I'm handling my problems by closing my credit card accounts and I've set up payment arrangements with all my creditors" than it is to say "You know, I've been meaning to get a handle on this problem, but my friends and I have been planning this trip to Mexico and I was going to charge it. . . ."

One veteran recruiter in Chicago gave the best advice for those with shaky finances:

> Don't wait for me to point out your problems and tell you what to do
> to get your life in shape. If your problems are that obvious to us and
> to everyone else who knows you, then you need to get your life in
> order before you start our process. Fix what you can and be ready to
> talk about the rest.

Community Involvement

This is one area where those who have little life experience can play catch-up. You may not have held many full-time jobs (if any), but you have had plenty of time to get involved with the world around you. Those of you who haven't already done so, get out there and volunteer for activities that will put you in contact with people of all types and ages. If you like kids and sports, help coach a Little League baseball team or a Peewee Football team. These experiences will provide you with an answer when the oral board asks you to describe a time when you helped others or when they ask about your leadership experience.

Suppose you are good with numbers and you like helping elderly people. Contact your local IRS office to see what kinds of volunteer programs exist to help older men and women with their tax forms. You'll certainly like how volunteering makes you feel. . . and, yes, the board will ask you that, too! The more involved you get, the more life experience you'll build and the more points you will win with your future employer.

Character

As you've read in previous chapters, law enforcement professionals are held to a higher personal standard. Your thoughts, opinions, past deeds, and experiences with friends, family, and coworkers all will be closely scrutinized by background investigators and by those who have the final authority to hire you. There's no room for those who can't take responsibility for their actions or tell the truth. And lying about anything during the hiring process will almost certainly get you disqualified, no matter what kind of excuse you present. (You'll hear more on this issue later in the chapter.)

All the professionals we polled agreed that no one expects you to be perfect and not to have made mistakes in your life, but you are expected to own up to them and to have learned from them. As old-fashioned as it may sound, employers want to hire men and women who will bring honor to the profession. Sheriff Don Farley of the Rockingham County Sheriff's Department sums it up:

> I expect any law enforcement officer to perform their duties in a professional manner that will earn the respect of those they serve. A person who wears the uniform is a representative of the people who demand a safe and secure place to work and raise a family. It is every officer's charge to perform his or her job and to live their personal life in a manner that is an example of what is right.

You've heard the comments we've culled from those in the know. Now it's time to formulate a strategy.

PLAN A—FOR THOSE IN HIGH SCHOOL OR RECENT HIGH SCHOOL GRADUATES

Your plan is simple:

- stay out of trouble: use your common sense, good judgment, and work on that college degree
- be careful with the checkbook and credit cards; pay your bills on time
- when you get a job, do your best: show up on time; treat your boss, coworkers, and the public with respect; build a reputation you'll be proud to talk about with your future employer
- get involved with your community by volunteering

PLAN B–FOR THE MORE EXPERIENCED APPLICANT

See Plan A! Being an older, more experienced applicant can be either an advantage or a disadvantage, but we'll talk more about this later in the chapter. What your history reveals about you will dictate where you end up. While you are putting Plan A to work for you, add these steps to it:

Identify your problems and work on them

- Financial problems? Seek advice from financial experts. Free advice and help is out there for the taking. Get copies of your credit report and identify your problem areas!
- Personal problems? Get those self-improvement projects under way. If this means getting professional counseling, pick up the phone and make an appointment—it's a sign of maturity, not weakness.
- Legal problems? Fix the ones you can, and be prepared to explain the rest. Consult an attorney to figure out your options.

Take off the blinders

- Take a long look at yourself and your past experiences. Get to know your strengths and weakness. Find out what people think about you and get them to tell you about areas in which you need improvement. Sound painful? It may be, but you'll be better prepared to talk about your faults with a hiring panel. Don't forget to tell them about your strengths! They are just as important as your weaknesses.
- If the word "nomad" describes your lifestyle, start compiling a list of former residences and jobs now. You'll appreciate the head start when it comes time to fill out your application.

Ready for Action

When you've done all you can do to make yourself as irresistible as possible to your future employer, the real work begins! No groaning—it's not as bad as all that. What you are about to read will reinforce some of the tips you've already learned, and the rest will give you a plan for how to handle what you didn't know about the most crucial phases in the hiring process: the Personal History Statement and the Oral Interview Boards.

THE PERSONAL HISTORY STATEMENT

The Personal History Statement is exactly that—a detailed personal statement of your life history. You may hear it called many things: the Application and the Applicant History Statement are the other common terms. No doubt you will come up with a few names of your own by the time you finish this project. Although the paperwork may go by different names, the reason for jumping through these hoops is the same. The purpose of the statement is to provide law enforcement background investigators with the material for a panel, an individual, or a personnel department to make a sound decision about hiring you. This section explores the quirks, subtleties, and realities of one of the most crucial phases of the application process.

Not for the Faint of Heart

When you take your first look at the Personal History Statement, you might want to be sitting down. This document can be daunting for the unprepared. All of your precious time, energy, and resources will be wasted if you aren't prepared to be asked about the tiniest details of your life. Not all employers require the same level of detail, but don't be surprised to find yourself hunting for the address of the kindergarten you attended.

Some agencies aren't so demanding. They'll ask you to start out with your high school days and work forward. However, it's best to expect the worst. As one investigator told an applicant to the Austin Police Department in Austin, Texas, "By the time I'm finished going through the information in this document, I'll know whether or not you were breast fed as a child." He was.

This Size Fits All

No matter where you choose to apply, this chapter may be the helping hand you need to make your background investigation go as smoothly as possible. It will serve as a guide to help you present an accurate, HONEST summary of your past and present life. After all, the Personal History Statement—how you complete it, what you reveal, and what you don't reveal—can determine whether or not you get the opportunity to convince an oral board you are worth hiring.

At first, you may not make the connection between the oral interview board and the Personal History Statement. The connection is there, and it's strong. What you reveal, or fail to reveal, in your Personal History Statement will come back around to help or haunt you at your oral board. Background investigators will poke around your life's basement using this document as a flashlight. They'll illuminate the good things and the bad things for all the oral board members to see and to use in their questioning. If you are forewarned, then you are forearmed.

Different Methods—Same Results

One of the more frustrating aspects of searching for that perfect law enforcement job is realizing that every local, state, and federal agency has its own way of doing business. Different law enforcement agencies rarely have the same priorities, budgets, staffing, or expectations for applicants. As a result, the process of hiring varies from one agency to another.

Be flexible. No matter how the application process is designed, or in what order you handle each task, the information you will need to supply to each department remains the same. They all want to know about your past, present, and potential.

No Need to Wait

Even if you haven't decided where to apply, you can start now. Make a list of every address you've lived at from the day you were born until the present. If you are 34 years old and normally change addresses twice a year you can pause a moment now to take a deep breath. Make this list and keep plenty of copies; this way you'll only need to do it once instead of every time you apply to a different department.

Addresses aren't the only project you can work on ahead of time. Create a list of every part-time and full-time job you've had since your working life began. Once again, not every department will use the same starting point to investigate your job history. Many will ask that you to list the jobs you've held during the past ten years; some will want your employment history from the past five years; and the others will want your history from the moment you received your first paycheck. With a list already in hand, you'll be ahead of the game.

And There's Always . . .

Tickets. Here's yet another project to work on before applying to an agency. Research your driving history. You'll be asked by some departments to list every traffic ticket you've ever received in any state or country, whether on a military post or on civilian roadways. Some may ask you to list only moving violations (these include speeding, running red lights, unsafe lane changes, etc.), while other departments want to see both moving violations and tickets for expired license plates, failure to wear seat belts, and expired automobile insurance, etc. One agency may ask about the tickets you've received in the past five years, while others may want to know your driving history from the first moment your foot touched the accelerator. Do your homework, and don't omit tickets you think they won't find, because that kind of ticket doesn't exist. Tickets leave paper trails and paper trails are the easiest kind of trails to follow.

Find These ASAP

Your pre-application preparations wouldn't be complete without a list of documents you'll need to have handy. This list does not include every form you may have to dig up, but it's a certainty your future employer will want to see a:

1. birth certificate
2. social security card
3. DD 214 (if you are a veteran)
4. naturalization papers (if applicable)
5. high school diploma or G.E.D. certificate
6. high school transcripts
7. college transcripts
8. current driver's license(s)
9. current copies of driving records
10. current consumer credit reports

If you don't have certified copies of these documents, start calling or writing the proper authorities now to find out how to get them. If you've sucked your social security card up in the vacuum cleaner and haven't seen it since, go to the social security office in your community and arrange for a new one. Legal documents often take anywhere from six to eight weeks for delivery, but you probably don't have that much time if you have already received and started on your Personal History Statement. Most departments have a deadline for filling out and returning Personal History Statements, so don't waste any time.

If time runs out and you realize you won't be able to submit the Personal History Statement with all the required documents, ask the powers-that-be what you should do. Many departments will tell you to attach a memo to your application outlining your problem and what you have done about it. For example, you've ordered a copy of your birth certificate but either the postal service is using it for scratch paper or your request is mired in the bureaucratic process. Attach a letter of explanation to your application detailing when you requested a copy of your birth certificate, where you asked for the copy to be sent, and when you expect to receive the document. Attach copies of all the correspondence you sent requesting a copy of your certificate, if you have them. That will show that you are making all the necessary efforts.

Check First

You have a little homework to do before collecting all of these documents. Check with as many departments as you can to find out what rules they have for how each document should be submitted (like college transcripts, for instance). Departmental officials may require you to have the school send the documentation directly to their recruiting office instead of to your home. The same goes for credit reports or copies of driving records. It's best to call the recruiting department, explain to them that you are trying to gather all of your documentation, and ask them how they require these documents to be delivered so you'll know what to do.

Other questions you need to ask are:

1. Do they need photocopies or original documents?
2. Will they return my original if I send it?
3. How recent does the credit history have to be?
4. What's the most recent copy they will accept of my college transcript?

The answers to these questions can save you money on postage. You'd be surprised at the number of ways each department can invent with for you to chase paper.

Ready for Action

You're as prepared as you can be. You've made your decision on where you are applying. Let's even assume you are at the point in the application process where you've received the Personal History Statement. Before you set pen to paper, make several copies of this form. Do not write on it, breathe on it, or set it down on the coffee table without FIRST having made a copy. After you have made copies, put away the original. You'll be using the photocopy as a working draft and a place to make mistakes. Eventually, you will transfer all the information from the practice copy onto the original. You may be spending lots of time on this project and using more than a few dimes in the copy machine before this is all over, but it will be time and money well spent. Especially if the unthinkable happens. And the unthinkable usually goes like this:

Your phone rings. It's your recruiter:

> Gee, Fred, this is Jones in recruiting and I have a little bad news. We can't seem to put a finger on that application you sent. Isn't that the darndest thing? Could you make us a copy from the one you have at home and send it out right away?

Don't think it doesn't happen. Be sure to make copies of the application and any accompanying documentation you submit, and keep them in a safe place. Hold on to these copies! You need to review this documentation before the oral board interiew, not to mention the possibility that you may need this information to complete other applications for other adventures years down the road.

Personal History Statements may vary from department to department, but the questions asked about these tedious documents have changed little over the years. The following are a few questions and comments made by actual applicants as they went through the process. The responses made to these questions and comments will allow you to learn from other people's mistakes, thereby giving you an advantage over the competition—and having an advantage can never hurt!

"What do you mean you don't accept resumes? It cost me $60 to get this one done!"

A formal resume (like one you may prepare for a civilian job) may not be much good to a law enforcement agency, depending on where you apply. Criminal justice instructors in many colleges suggest to their students to have a resume made, and that's not bad advice. However, it's always best to call and ask a recruiter whether or not his or her agency accepts them. Why go to the expense if the agency is going to throw away the resume upon receipt? Most agencies will rely upon their Personal History Statements to get the details of your life, education, and experience, so save yourself time and dimes when you can.

"I didn't realize the Personal History Statement would take so long to complete and the deadline for turning it in caught me by surprise. I got in a hurry and left some things blank."

The letter this applicant received in the mail disqualifying her from further consideration probably caught her by surprise as well. As you know from reading this chapter, the Personal History Statement requires planning, efficiency, and attention to detail. Most departments demand accuracy, thoroughness, and timeliness. There are many applicants to choose from who have taken the time to properly complete the application; why shoud a busy background investigator bother with an applicant who has left half the form blank? In fact, many departments will tell you in their application instructions that failing to respond to questions or to provide requested information will result in disqualification.

"I read most of the instructions. I didn't see the part that said I had to print."

Read all of the instructions. Every sentence. Every word. And please do so before you begin filling out your practice copy of the Personal History Statement. In fact, you need to read the entire document from the first page to the last before you tackle this project. Have a note pad next to you and as you read make notes of every question you do not understand. You'll be making a phone call to your recruiter AFTER reading the entire document to ask questions. It's important to read the whole document because your questions may be answered as you continue to read. It's embarrassing to call with a question that the recruiter answers by saying "Well, as you would have found out by reading the next sentence, you should. . . ."

"No one is going to follow up on all this stuff anyway. It'd take way too long and it's way too involved."

A good background investigator lives for the opportunity to follow up on the details of your life. That's their job. They must sign their name at the bottom of the report documenting their investigation. It's not wise to assume that someone will put his or her career at risk by doing a sloppy job on your background investigation. A thorough investigator will take as much time as is needed to do a good job. The good news is that you can earn brownie points by making that investigator's job as simple as possible. Give them as much information as you possibly can and make that information ACCURATE. When you write down a phone number, make sure it's correct. For example, if you used to work at Jumpin' Jacks Coffee Parlor four years ago and you still remember the phone number, CALL that number to make sure it's correct before you write it down. Nothing is more irritating to a busy investigator than dialing wrong number after wrong number. If you only have one phone number for an old employer and you discover it's no longer in service, make a note of it so the investigator doesn't assume you are being lazy or evasive. Phone numbers get changed and businesses close every day.

When you turn in the Personal History Statement you are building upon the reputation you founded the moment you first made contact with recruiting staff.

An application that is turned in on time, filled out neatly and meticulously, and has correct, detailed information that is easily verified says a lot about the person who submitted it. Not only will an investigator have warm fuzzy thoughts for anyone who makes his or her job easier, he or she will come to the conclusion that you will carry these same traits into your law enforcement work.

The investigator, the oral board, and the staff psychologist all will be looking at HOW you filled out the application as well as what information is contained within. They'll build a case for hiring (or not hiring) you based on facts, impressions, and sometimes even intuition. With this in mind, every detail is worth a second look before you declare your Personal History Statement complete. Ask yourself:

+ Is my handwriting as neat as it can be?
+ Did I omit answers or leave blanks?
+ Do my sentences make sense?
+ Is my spelling correct?
+ Are my dates and times consistent?

"I figured you could find out that information easier than I could. That's why I didn't look up that information. After all, you're the investigator."

This applicant is probably still looking for a job. The Personal History Statement is a prime opportunity for you to showcase your superb organizational skills, knack for detail, and professionalism. Do as much of the work as you can for the background investigator. Make extra credit points. For example, let's say you worked for Grace's High Heels and Muffler Emporium. The business closed after a few months (much to everyone's surprise) and you moved on to other employment. You're not sure what became of Grace, your immediate supervisor and owner of the business, but you do know a friend of hers. Contact that friend, find out Grace's address and phone number, and give this information to your investigator. Yes, the investigator could find Grace on his or her own, but you went the extra mile, you showed the initiative, and you are going to get the brownie points for it.

It's not uncommon for a law enforcement agency to get thousands of applications per year. Most of the applicants have the same credentials to offer as you do. Do all you can do to stand out from the crowd. Nothing gets noticed faster than efficiency, professionalism, and accuracy. Well, that's not quite true: Inaccuracies, sloppiness, and laziness usually draw first notice.

"I know I got disqualified, but it's only because I misunderstood the question. I didn't want to ask about it because I didn't want to look dumb."

If you do not understand a question, ASK someone. By not making sure you know how to properly answer a question, you run the risk of answering it incorrectly, incompletely, or not at all. Any of these mistakes can lead to your disqualification if an investigator thinks you are not telling the truth, or that you are unwilling to provide the information requested. Don't take chances when a simple question will clear up the confusion.

"You know, I didn't have any idea what that question meant so I just guessed."

Never guess. Never assume. This advice cannot be repeated too often. If you don't know, find out. ASK QUESTIONS. Answering them is part of the job of recruiters and background investigators.

"I lied because I thought if I told the truth, I'd look bad."

Never lie about anything. As far as law enforcement professionals are concerned, there is no such thing as a harmless lie. Supervisors don't want people working for them who cannot tell the truth, no one wants to work with partners whom they can't trust, and communities expect *criminals* to lie, not officers, agents, and deputies! Your credibility must be beyond reproach.

Let's look at an example. One applicant told his recruiter that the reason he didn't admit to getting a ticket for failure to have his car registered was because he thought the department would think he wasn't organized and couldn't take care of business. Which would you prefer for a potential employer to know about you: that you lie instead of admitting to mistakes, or that you make mistakes and admit to them?

"I listed John Doe as a personal reference because he's the mayor and I worked on his campaign. Why did my investigator call and make me give another reference?"

Choose your personal references carefully. Background investigators do not want to talk to references because they have impressive credentials. They want to talk to them so they can get a feel for who you are as a person. Investigators will know within minutes whether or not a reference knows you well. (Personal references are important enough to warrant their own in-depth discussion later in this chapter.)

How To Read and Answer Questions

Reading questions and instructions carefully is crucial to successfully completing the Personal History Statement. Certain words should leap off the page. These are the words on which you should focus:

- all
- every
- any
- each

If you see these words in a question, you are being asked to include all the information you know. For example, you may see the following set of instructions in your Personal History Statement:

List any and all pending criminal charges against you.

This doesn't mean list the charges facing you in Arizona, but not the ones in Nevada. This department wants to know about every single criminal charge that may be pending against you no matter in what parish, village, city, county, country, or planet you are being charged. Do not try to tap dance your way around instructions like these for any reason. If your fear is that the information you reveal may make you look bad, you may have some explaining to do. And you may have perfectly good explanations for your past and present. If you lie or try to dishonestly make yourself look good, you'll be disqualified in short order, and no one will get the opportunity to consider your explanations.

Another question you may see is:

Have you ever been arrested or taken into police custody for any reason?

The key words are ever and any. This question means at any time in your life, beginning with your birth, and up to and including the second that just went by. If you don't know what is meant by the term "arrested," then call your recruiter or investigator and ASK. Do not play the well-no-one-put-handcuffs-on-me-so-I-wasn't-really-arrested game. When in doubt, list any situation you think could possibly fall into the category on which you are working. The best advice is ASK IF YOU DON'T KNOW!

Here's a request for information that includes several key words:

List all traffic citations (moving and non-moving), excluding parking tickets, you received in the past five (5) years, in this or any other state.

In this example, the request is very clear. What you should do is make a complete list of every kind of violation for which you've been issued a citation in the past five years, no matter where you got it or what the traffic violation was. They even let you know the one type of citation they don't want—parking tickets. If you aren't sure what constitutes a moving violation or non-moving violation, call the department and have them explain. Keep in mind that when the officer issued you a citation, that single piece of paper may have contained more than one violation. Most citations have blanks for at least three violations. For example, last year you were pulled over for speeding. The officer discovered you had no insurance and your car license plates were expired. She told you she was writing you three tickets for these violations, but handed you only one piece of paper. Did you get one citation or three? You got three.

Once again, ASK if you don't know. No one will make fun of you if you are unfamiliar with terminology such as "moving violation."

Personal References

Your personal references are the people who will be able to give the background investigator the best picture of you as a whole person. Some Personal History Statements ask you to list at least five people as references; some only ask for three. You also may be given a specific time limit for how long you have to have known these people before listing them. For example, your instructions may direct you to list only those individuals whom you've known for a minimum of two years. If there are instructions for this section, pay close attention to them. Selecting your references is not something you should take lightly.

Earlier, you learned that by making the investigator's job easier, you make the application process run more smoothly, you get brownie points, and your background check is finished quickly. The Personal References Section is one area where you really want to make the investigator's job easy. You'll want the investigator to talk to people who know you well, who can comment on your hobbies, interests, personality, and ability to interact with others. Try to choose friends who will be honest, open, and sincere. When an investigator calls a reference and finds that the person he or she is talking to barely has an idea of who you are, red flags will spring up. Investigators are suspicious by nature. The investigator will wonder why you listed someone who doesn't know you well. Are you afraid someone who knows you well will reveal information you don't want revealed? This is how an investigator will look at the situation. And, at the very least, you'll get a phone call requesting another reference because the one listed was unsatisfactory.

Most investigators assume you will tell personal references that they have been listed and that they will be getting a phone call or a personal visit from the investigating agency. Give *correct* phone numbers, find out from your references what times they are most accessible, and *especially* find out if they have any objections to being contacted. You don't want a reluctant personal reference; they often do more harm than good.

Tell your references how important it is for them to be open and honest with the investigator. Let them know that if they do not understand a question, they should feel free to tell the investigator they don't understand. It's also wise to let them know that there are no right or wrong answers to these questions. Investigators do not want to have a conversation with someone who is terrified of saying the "wrong thing." And that's what your personal references should expect to have with an investigator—a conversation, not an interrogation. Your goal here is to let the investigator see you as a person through the eyes of those who know you best.

Looks Aren't Everything—Or Are They?

You've filled out your practice copy of the Personal History Statement, made all your mistakes, answered all the questions, and filled in all the appropriate blanks. Now you're ready to make the final copy.

Part of the impression you will make on those who have the hiring and firing power will come from the appearance of your application. Is your handwriting so sloppy that investigators pass your work around to see who can decipher it? Did you follow the instructions directing you to PRINT? Were you too lazy to attach an additional sheet of paper instead of writing up and down the sides of the page? Did you spell words correctly? Do your sentences make sense to the reader? (Here is a good tip: read your answers out loud to yourself. If it doesn't make sense to your own ears, then you need to re-work what you wrote.)

Each contact you have with the hiring agency makes an impression. The written impression you make with your Personal History Statement is one that will follow you through the entire process. In fact, it can have a bearing on whether or not you make it into the academy, because most departments score you on the document's appearance.

Here are some items you might find useful as you work on your application:

1. a dictionary
2. a grammar handbook
3. a good pen (or pencil—whichever the directions tell you to use)
4. a healthy case of paranoia

The paranoia will ensure that you not only check and recheck your own work, but also have someone you trust check it before you make your final copy.

You now have the information you'll need to make the Personal History Statement a manageable task. This is not a document to take lightly, especially now that you are aware of the power this document has over your potential career. Remember, it's important that you:

- carefully follow instructions
- be honest and open about your past and present
- provide accurate information
- choose excellent personal references
- turn in presentable, error-free documentation
- submit all documents on time

A law enforcement agency can ask for nothing better than an applicant who takes this kind of care and interest in the application process. You will appreciate what all this hard work does for your oral interview experience!

THE ORAL INTERVIEW BOARDS

"Welcome to the board." If someone says those words to you, you've passed a large part of the process and are one step closer to your dream. The law enforcement oral interview board, no matter who conducts it or what form it takes, is unlike any oral job interview you will ever experience. The questions are pointed, personal, and uncompromising. Vague, plastic responses will usually goad the panel into rougher questioning until they get the honest response they seek. The next section will show you how to prepare for the oral board from the moment you apply until the head of the board thanks you for your participation.

Hire Me, Please!

If you are like most people, you've had some experience asking someone for a job. So, it's not unrealistic to expect that an oral interview board will be similar to a civilian oral interview—or is it? Yes and no; there are a few similarities. Both prospective civilian and law enforcement employers are looking for the most qualified person for the job: reliable, honest, hardworking, dependable men and women.

"Hire" Expectations

Civilian employers, just like law enforcement employers, expect applicants to show up on time for their interviews, dressed professionally, and flaunting their best manner. When you enter a law enforcement oral interview board, however, you will realize that the interviewers have more than a superficial interest in you and your past experiences. The board will also have more than a two-page resume in their hands when the interview begins.

Exactly who will be using the details of your personal and professional lives to interview you? It will be a panel of two, three, or four (maybe more) individuals with one purpose in mind: to learn everything they can about you. Some agencies have civilian personnel specialists on their boards, but most interview boards will be made up of experienced law enforcement officers.

These board members will be using the information provided on your Personal History Statement and the information investigators discovered during their background check. The investigators will provide board members with a detailed report on your past and present life history. Yes, you'll be asked both questions to which the board members already know the answer, and questions to which they don't know the answers. You'll be asked to explain why you've made the decisions you've made in your life—both personal and professional. You'll also be asked questions that don't have right or wrong answers. In short, you can expect an intense grilling from men and women who don't have the time or patience for applicants who come to their interview unprepared.

Tell What You Know, Know What You Tell

Before you reach the interview stage of the application process, you will have filled out the Personal History Statement (aka the Applicant History Statement, or simply the Application). Don't underestimate its role in the oral interview. The Personal History Statement guides the oral interview board through your past and present life. You must be willing to expose your life to the scrutiny of the board by giving them an informative, ACCURATE tour of where you've been and who you are.

Since the Personal History Statement is the guide that background investigators use to conduct their investigation and is what their final report to the board is based upon, you should make that document the focus of your life when you are filling it out. Members of the oral board are given a copy of your Personal History Statement, and a copy of the investigators' final report on you. While you are answering questions for the board, most board members will be shuffling through the pages of your statement, checking what you say against what you have written. Naturally, you'll want to remember the information you gave them on your Personal History Statement. Instead of tossing and turning the night before your interview, spend your time reading and rereading your Personal History Statement so that you know what they know about you.

How much effort you put into the Personal History Statement will have a direct impact on how difficult your oral interview will be. If board members have an accurate, detailed picture of you as a whole person from the information you have supplied, your time under the microscope will be less than the applicant who turned in a vague, mistake-laden account of his or her past and present life. If the thought of the oral interview board makes your palms sweat, then pay close attention to the section on how to handle the Personal History Statement.

There's Plenty of Time, Right?

Preparation for the oral interview board should begin with the decision to apply. From the moment you first make contact with a law enforcement agency, everything you say and do will potentially raise questions for the oral interview board. Even when you walk through the doors of the recruiting office to pick up an application, you have the opportunity to make a lasting impression, because the professionals who deal with you are trained to notice and remember people and details.

If you arrive to pick up an application wearing your favorite cutoff jeans and trashed out, beer-stained T-shirt, you may be shocked several months later when a board member asks you why you chose to make that particular fashion statement. Dress as neatly and professionally as possible for each and every time you make visual contact with the department where you want to work.

The same goes for telephone calls—when you contact a department to request an application, you will make an impression on the person who answers the phone. As silly as it may make you feel, it's a good idea to rehearse what you say before you dial. In fact, it's not a bad idea to write down what you'd like to say before you call. This will give you control over the impression you make and eliminate the possibility of your first words being: "uh... hi... I... uh... wanna... uh... Can you mail me a... uh... one of those... uh... I wanna be an FBI agent but I need a... application! Yeah, that's it!"

Do the same for any questions you may have. Make a list of questions and as you ask each one, listen carefully to the response without interruption. Above all, never ask a question that is designed to show off how much you know. The chances of you knowing more about law enforcement than the person who is already working in the field is slim. Your opportunity to impress the agency will come later in an appropriate setting—the oral interview board.

Self-Awareness—Don't Show Up Without It!

You wouldn't show up for a car race on a tricycle, any more than you would want to put out a fire with gasoline. Using this same logic, it's safe to say that you'd never sit down in front of a panel of professionals (who may or may not offer you a career dealing with people) without good self-awareness.

Self-awareness is knowing yourself: being aware of what you do and why you do it. Many of the questions you'll hear from the board are designed to reveal how well you know yourself and how honest you can be about your talents and your shortcomings.

Big Tip!

Do NOT pay any attention to consultants or books suggesting that you downplay, or deny having, weaknesses. If you remember only one piece of advice from this chapter, please let it be this! If an oral board member asks you to list weaknesses and you cannot think of any, he or she will be more than happy to use your Pesonal History Statement to illustrate any weaknesses you aren't able to identify.

You should be able to list your weaknesses with the same unhesitating manner with which you list your strengths. You should also be able to tell the board what you are doing to correct or compensate for those weaknesses. If you truly aren't aware of your failings, ask trusted friends and relatives to name them for you. Write down what you think your weaknesses are and then compare your list with what your friends and family have said. Don't forget to ask them about your strengths as well. Some applicants find talking about strengths as difficult as talking about weaknesses. You must be able to do both without hesitation.

Don't You Remember? YOU Put It On Your Application!

Part of being self-aware is knowing what others know about you. Few of the questions during your oral board interview should come as a surprise if you have taken the time to re-read your Personal History Statement.

Before arriving for the board you must take the time to review your application and to carefully think about each piece of information. The questions posed by the board are generated mostly from the information you supply on the Personal History Statement. As you review your copy of the statement, think about possible questions such information could generate.

For example, if one of the questions on the application directed you to list any instances when you've been fired from a job, think about how you would respond if you were asked: "Mr. Smith, can you tell the board why you were fired from Tread Lightly Tire Shop in 1993?" Although you may have previously told the investigator why you were fired, the board will want to hear it for themselves.

Help Yourself!

Conquer Public Speaking Fears

Being interviewed by a group of people is a lot like having a nightmare in which you show up at work in nothing but a pair of socks. You'll experience anxiety, sweaty palms, and a burning desire to be someplace else. Public speaking classes will help ease the fear of speaking in front of groups.

Strongly consider taking a speech class at a nearby community college or through an adult education course. At the very least, have a friend ask you questions about yourself and have them take notes about any annoying mannerisms you may exhibit while speaking. Then practice your speaking skills and learn to control those mannerisms.

Practice is one of the keys to success for an oral board interview. If you've ever truly practiced something—batting a ball, for instance—you know that once you have the motion down you can rely on your muscles to "remember" what to do when it comes time to play. The same rationale holds true for practicing oral board answers.

One effective technique is to mentally place yourself in a situation and visualize how you want to act or respond when the pressure is on. Some professionals call this mental exercise "What if. . . ," and they use this technique to formulate a plan of action for those times when split-second decisions are needed. Visualizing a successful performance can help trigger that response once you're in the actual situation. This technique will work for you if you practice, practice, practice.

Not on Time? Tsk, Tsk!

Show the board how much you want this job. They'll check to see when you arrived. An early arrival shows you planned ahead for emergencies (flat tires, wrong turns, etc.), that you arrived in enough time to prepare yourself mentally for what you are about to do, and that you place as much value on other people's time as on your own.

Packaging Sells a Product

You may feel like you don't have much control over what happens to you in an oral interview setting, but there is one area in which you have total control. The initial impression you make on board members is in your hands, and it is the perfect opportunity to score points without even opening your mouth. The way you dress sends a signal to the people who are watching as you walk into the room.

Blue jeans and a "nice shirt" tell the board you wouldn't mind having the job if someone would give it to you. On the other hand, business suits (for men and women) tell the board that you want this job, you take this interview seriously, and there's nothing casual about the way you are approaching it. If you don't own a suit, borrow, rent, or buy one, and wear it! You've already invested time and money in the education needed for most criminal justice jobs. This is not the time to balk at spending a few dollars more on appropriate clothing.

Make Mama Proud

After you've earned points with your professional appearance, it's time to earn more points with your manners. Most law enforcement agencies are paramilitary organizations—your first clue should be the uniforms and the rank-based structure. In the military it's customary to address higher-ranking men and women with courtesy. "Yes, ma'am," "yes, sir," "no, ma'am," and "no, sir," are the responses expected from military personnel. If you have military experience you will be ahead in this area.

If you are not accustomed to using these terms of courtesy, practice them! Make a conscious effort to use them every day. It's rarely considered rude to simply respond "yes" or "no" to a question, but you'll be on shaky ground if "yeah" or "uh-huh" are your customary responses.

Location can be important. If you've flown from New York to Texas to apply for a job, you definitely do not want to say "yeah" or "what?" in your interview. Southerners raise their children to say "yes, ma'am" and "no, sir"; hearing "huh?" or "yeah" is at best an irritant to Southern ears. This may not be an issue in other parts of the nation, although it's best to assume many board members have either been in the military or like the paramilitary structure of law enforcement.

No doubt you realize that an oral interview board sees many, many applicants when a department is in the hiring phase. Most boards typically schedule five or six interviews each day. Some departments schedule interviews one day a week, while other departments have interviews every day of the week. You may be talking to people who are quite tired of listening. That means the "little things" take on an extra importance.

Yes, It All Matters

What you've read so far may seem inconsequential. This is far from the truth. You walk a fine line when you appear before an oral interview board. You should appear self-confident and poised, not cocky or arrogant. You're expected to be nervous, but not so nervous that you can't communicate beyond an occasional grunt or nod. You're expected to be polite, but not to fawn all over the board. Above all, you are expected to be yourself, and not who you imagine the board might want you to be. Which brings up another point: What exactly is the board looking for in an applicant?

People Talent—A Must

Law enforcement professionals today are expected to be highly responsive to the public. Agency officers are looking for applicants who have excellent verbal skills and a strong desire to "be there" for the public. It's not a secret that the successful applicant will need superior people-handling skills. But what about other skills?

Oral interview boards are faced with the formidable task of hiring individuals who have the skills and talents equal to the demands of modern law enforcement. The most highly sought-after individuals are those who are good with people and who can handle the demands of advanced technology. Computers are here to stay. If you think a keyboard is a piece of wood on which you hang patrol car keys, you are in for a surprise. You can be sure that your competition is in class hunched over a keyboard at this very moment, because they know oral interview boards love to hear "Why, certainly" in response to the question: "Have you ever used a computer?" If you haven't already, now is the time to brush up on your typing skills and sign up for a computer class.

Liability is another issue. Lawsuits and threats of lawsuits have law enforcement agencies scrambling to find applicants who have the qualities and skills that will keep them out of negative headlines and off the wrong side of civil suits.

Show Your Stuff

Law enforcement agencies want it all. There's always room for men and women who can leap tall buildings and do the speeding train thing, but even if your cape isn't red, you can still compete if you can convince the board you have the following qualities:

- maturity
- common sense
- good judgment
- compassion
- integrity
- honesty
- reliability
- the ability to work without constant supervision

These qualities aren't ranked in order of importance because it would be impossible to determine which is most important. They are all important in the eyes of the board, and your task in the oral interview is to convince the board that you have all these qualities. Since you are in a question-and-answer setting, do your convincing by how you respond and what you say to questions.

Youth and Inexperience—a Plus or Minus?

The question here is will an oral board think you have enough life experience for them to be willing to take a chance on hiring you. Law enforcement agencies have never been as liability-conscious as they are today. Incidents like the Rodney King Trial and subsequent Los Angeles riots have heightened the liability awareness of law enforcement agencies around the country.

This concern haunts personnel, recruiters, background investigators, oral interview boards, and everyone who has anything to do with deciding who gets a badge. The first question you hear when trouble arises is: "How did that person get hired here anyway?" As a result, agencies are scrutinizing applicants more closely than ever before and they are leaning toward individuals who have proven track records in employment, academics, volunteer work, and community involvement.

However, what you read earlier in this chapter is true: youth and inexperience are not going to disqualify you from the process. You should be aware, though, that if you are 21 years old and have never held a job or been financially independent, you will have a more difficult time getting hired on your first try than someone who has job references to check and who is able to demonstrate a history of reliability, responsibility, and community involvement.

Maturity is a major concern of law enforcement agencies. They cannot afford to hire men and women who are unable to take responsibility for their actions or, in some cases, the actions of those around them. Since maturity cannot be measured in terms of age, agencies will want to see as much proof as possible that you have sufficient maturity and enough potential to risk hiring you.

Get Out in the World

Make it as easy as possible for the board to see how well you handle responsibility. Sign up for volunteer work now if you don't have any experience dealing with people. If you are still living at home with your parents, be able to demonstrate the ways in which you are responsible to them. If you are on your own, but living with roommates, talk to the board about this experience and how it has helped you to learn to handle conflict.

You may want to work extra hard on your communication skills before going to the board. If you are young, you will be able to better sell yourself to the board the more articulate you are. As a younger applicant, you will have a greater need to be open and allow the board see you as a worthy investment.

Older and Wiser Pays Off

Being an older applicant certainly is not a hindrance. Boards are receptive to men and women who have life experience that can be examined, picked apart, and verified. Maturity, mentioned before, is not necessarily linked to how old you are. Older applicants can be either blessed or cursed by the trail they've left in life.

Many older applicants have gone down in flames because they were unable to satisfactorily explain incidents in their past and present that revealed their immaturity and irresponsibility.

Applicants of any age who have listed a great number of jobs or have submitted Personal History Statements too thick to run through a stapling machine should be extra-vigilant about doing their homework before the interview. If you fall into this category, you should carefully re-examine the copy of the application used by your background investigator. Be fully aware of any problem areas and know what you will most likely be asked to explain. Decide now what you are going to say. Prepare, prepare, prepare.

Don't Leave The Meter Running

The longer your history, the longer you can expect to sit before an oral interview board. If a board is not required to adhere to time limits, you may endure a longer session than other applicants simply because you have more material to cover. The more you know about yourself and the more open you are about your life, the smoother your interview will run. This advice holds true for all applicants, regardless of age.

Questions—The Nitty-Gritty

What kind of questions are they going to ask? Isn't that what everyone is really worried about when they are sitting in the chair labeled "NEXT" outside of the interview room? You will hear all kinds of questions—questions about your family life, questions about your likes and dislikes, questions about your temperament, your friends, and even a few designed to make you laugh so you'll get a little color back into your face. There won't be many questions that can be answered with simply "yes" or "no" because you won't get that lucky. Let's look at the types of questions you are likely to hear.

Open-Ended Questions

The open-ended question is the one you are most likely to be asked. An example of an open-ended question is:

> **Board Member:** "Mr. Jones, can you tell the board about your Friday-night bowling league?"

Board members like these questions because it gives them an opportunity to see how articulate you can be and how you think. This is also a way for them to ease into more specific questions. For example:

Board Member: "Mr. Jones, can you tell the board about your Friday-night bowling league?"

Jones: "Yes ma'am. I've been bowling in this league for about two years. We meet every Friday night around 6 p.m. and bowl until about 8:30 p.m. I like it because it gives me something to do with friends I may not otherwise get to see because everyone is so busy. It also gives me time to spend with my wife. We're in first place right now and I like it that way."

Board Member: "Oh, congratulations. You must be a pretty competitive bowler."

Jones: "Yes ma'am, I am. I like to win and I take the game pretty seriously."

Board Member: "How do you react when your team loses, Mr. Jones?"

That one series of questions generates enough information for the board to draw many conclusions about Mr. Jones. They can see that he likes to interact with his friends, that he thinks spending time with his wife is a high priority, and that competition and winning are important to him. Mr. Jones' answers open up an avenue for the board to explore how he reacts to disappointment, and if he is able to articulate his feelings and reactions. They'll get a good idea of his temperament.

Open-ended questions allow the board to fish around for information, but this is not a negative. You should seize these opportunities to open up to the board and give them an idea of who you are.

Obvious Questions

Everyone in the room already knows the answer to this type of question. For example:

Board Member: "Mr. Jones, you were in the military for four years?"

Jones: "Yes sir, I was in the Marines from 1982 until 1986."

Board Member: "Why did you leave?"

The obvious question is used as a way to give the applicant a chance to warm up and to be alerted to which area the board is about to explore. It's also a way for the board to verify the information they've been provided. Board members and background investigators can misread or misunderstand the information they receive. Being aware of this, board members will be careful to confirm details with you during the interview.

Fishing Expeditions

The fishing expedition question is always nerve-wracking to answer. You aren't certain why they are asking it or where it came from, and they aren't giving out any clues. For example:

Board Member: "Mr. Jones, in your application you stated that you've never been detained by police. (Usually they will pause for effect and then get to the point.) You've never been detained?"

If your nerves aren't wracked by this kind of questioning, someone probably needs to check you for a pulse. In the example above, if the applicant has been detained by police and has failed to list this on his application, then he'll be wondering if the board KNOWS this happened. The odds are very high that the board does indeed know the answer before it asks the question. If the applicant has never been detained then paranoia is certain to set in. Did someone on his list of references lie to the background investigator? Did someone on the board misread his application? These questions race through his mind as the board scrutinizes him.

Chances are, the board is simply fishing to see what he'll say. In any event, don't let these questions cause you a dilemma; if you are honest there can be no dilemma. You simply MUST tell the truth at ALL times in an oral board. At stake is your integrity, reputation, and, not least of all, your career. Don't try to guess WHY the board is asking a question. Your only job is to answer truthfully and openly.

Situational/Ethics Queries

Who doesn't dread these? You hear the words "What would you do if . . ." and your heart pounds wildly. For example:

> **Board Member:** "Mr. Jones, assume you are a police officer and you are on your way to back up another officer at the scene of a burglary at a clothing store. You walk in just in time to see him pick up a small bottle of men's cologne and put it into his pocket. What do you do?"

Some oral boards are almost exclusively one situational question after another. Other departments may ask one, then spend the rest of the interview asking you about your past job history. Your best defense is to decide ahead of time what your ethics are and go with how you honestly feel. The only possible right answer is your answer. If the board doesn't like what they hear then you may be grilled intensely about your answer; however, you should not assume that you've given a "wrong" answer if the board does begin questioning you more intensely. Boards have more than one reason for hammering away at you and it's never safe to assume why they are doing it.

Keep in mind, too, that it's not uncommon for one board member to be assigned the task of trying to get under an applicant's skin. The purpose of this is to see if the applicant rattles easily under pressure or loses his or her temper when baited. The person assigned this task is not hard to spot. He or she will be the one you'd love to push in front of a bus after he or she has asked such questions as: "Why in the world would we want to hire someone like YOU?"

Expect boards to jump on every discrepancy they hear and pick apart some of your comments—all because they want to see how you handle pressure. Not all departments designate a person to perform this function, but someone is usually prepared to slip into this role during the interview.

Role-Play Situations

Answering tough questions is stressful enough, but doing it under role-play conditions is even tougher. Many agencies are using this technique more and more frequently in the oral board interview. A board member will instruct you to pretend you are a law enforcement agent and ask you to act out your verbal and/or physical responses. For example:

> **Board Member:** "Mr. Jones, I want you to pretend that you are a
> police officer and you are chasing a fleeing suspect. The suspect is
> running from you now and I want you to stand up and instruct him
> to stop by yelling: 'Freeze! Police!'"

Board members may set up more elaborate role-playing scenes for you. Try
to enter these situations with a willingness to participate. Most people are aware
that you are not a professional actor or actress, so they are not looking for Academy Award-winning performances. Do the best you can. Role-playing is used heavily in almost all police academies and training situations today, so expect to do a
lot of it during your training as a law enforcement professional. Shy, reserved
people may have difficulty with this kind of interaction. Practice how you'd handle
this scene and prepare yourself mentally as best you can.

They Can't Ask Me That, Can They?

They, the members of the oral board, can indeed ask you just about any question that comes to mind. Applying for a job in public safety puts you in a different league than the civilian-sector applicant. Federal and state laws prohibit
civilian employers from seeking certain information about their applicants, but
law enforcement agencies are allowed greater freedom of inquiry for obvious
reasons.

For example, you'll rarely find a space for an applicant's birth date on an
application for employment in private industry. This is the result of age discrim-
ination litigation. However, law enforcement agencies, as well as other agencies
dealing with public safety, need such information to perform thorough background investigations, and therefore do not have the same restrictions. You will
be expected to provide your date of birth, race, and gender before you get very
far into the application process for any law enforcement agency. Because you are
applying for a sensitive public safety job, you should expect to provide highly
personal information.

In short, law enforcement agencies can ask you any question that has a bearing on your mental stability, your integrity, your honesty, your character, your
reputation in the community, and your ability to do the physical tasks common to
the job. If some of the questions are probing and perhaps even offensive, it is
because you are being held to a higher standard by both the courts (which allow
these questions to be asked), and the agencies that want to hire you to protect life
and property.

Answers—How Many Are There?

While you are sitting in the interview hot seat you may feel like only two kinds of answers exist—the one you wish you had given and the one you wish you could take back. There isn't a law enforcement officer today who doesn't have a war story about the one thing he wishes he hadn't brought up in his oral board interview. And this is to be expected. Nerves, pressure, and that random attack of stupidity often conspire at the most inopportune times. To help you be on guard for these moments, let's look at the elusive "right" and "wrong" answer.

The Right Answer

The answers the board wants to hear are the ones only you can give. They want your opinion, your reasons, your personal experiences, and they want to know what you would do under certain circumstances. If you try to say what you think the board wants to hear you will give them shallow, unsatisfying responses to their questions.

The Wrong Answer

The wrong answer to any question is the answer you think you should say because that's what you've been told the board wants to hear. Do not take well-meant advice from friends who haven't been before a board in the last five years or who can't remember much about the one they did go through. Boards will often over-look answers they don't like if they feel you have good reasons for what you say and if you are being honest with them.

If the board fails you, it will not be because you gave the wrong answer. It will be either because you are not the kind of person they were looking for, or because there were some things about your life or yourself that the board feels you need some time to work on before they'll consider you for a job in law enforcement.

What DO I Say?

It's not so much what you say as how you say it. The best way to answer any question is with directness, honesty, and brevity. Keep your answers short, but give enough information to fully answer the question. The board won't be handing out prizes for your way with words, but they also don't want to have to drag answers out of you in order to get enough information.

There are a few ways of answering questions you want to avoid. Try not to play "if you ask the question just the right way, I'll give you the right answer" with the board. For example:

Board Member: "Mr. Jones, I see you've been arrested once for public intoxication while you were in college? Is that true?"

Jones: "No, sir."

Board Member: "Really? That's odd. It says here on page seven that you were arrested and spent the night in the city jail."

Jones: "Yes, well, I wasn't exactly arrested because the officer didn't put handcuffs on me."

Don't play word games with the board. You won't win. In this case the applicant clearly knows that the board is aware of his arrest record, but he's trying to downplay the incident by ducking the question.

Then there's the "you can have the answer if you drag it out of me" technique, which you also want to avoid. For example:

Board Member: "Mr. Jones, tell the board why you left the job you held at Tread Lightly Tire Shop."

Jones: "I was fired."

Board Member: Why were you fired?"

Jones: "Because the boss told me not to come back."

Board Member: "Why did the boss tell you not to come back?"

Jones: "Because I was fired."

Board Member: "What happened to cause you to be fired?"

Jones: "I was rude."

Board Member: "Rude to whom and under what circumstances?"

You get the idea. This question could have been answered fully when the Board Member first asked Jones why he left the tire shop. The board would prefer that you not ramble when you answer questions, but they would also appreciate a little balance. This applicant runs the risk of being labeled a smart aleck with this kind of response. An oral board's patience is usually worn thin by an applicant who uses this answering technique.

Let's not forget the "you can have any answer but the one that goes with your question" technique. Avoid this one as well. For example:

> **Board Member:** "Well, Mr. Jones, we know about some of the things you are good at, now tell us something about yourself that you'd like to improve."

> **Jones:** "I'm really good with people. People like me and find it easy to talk to me for some reason. I guess it's because I'm such a good listener."

If he is a good listener, Mr. Jones didn't demonstrate it with that answer. It's important to listen to the question and answer directly. If you duck the question the board will assume you either have something to hide or are not being honest. If you don't understand how to answer the question, tell the person who asked it that you don't understand. They will be happy to rephrase the question or explain what they want. Be specific and above all, answer the question you were asked, not the one you wished you were asked.

The Final Roundup

Chances are the postal service is looking pretty good right about now. But don't let all of this information become overwhelming; make yourself step back and look at the big picture. You know what kind of overall impression you are likely to make. Cut yourself some slack. The people who interview you aren't perfect and they have no real desire to hire someone who is (considering they may have to work with you some day).

Keep your sense of humor intact while you're going through this process. Don't go into the board cracking jokes, but if you can keep your sense of humor close at hand you might actually be able to react if the board makes a joke. It wouldn't be unusual for this to happen. Most law enforcement personnel like to tease or joke around to relieve stress, but let the board lead the way.

Self-confidence is key. Relax, believe in yourself, and let it all come out naturally. If you feel like you are "blowing it" during the interview, show the board your self-confidence by stopping yourself, taking a deep breath, and telling them that's not exactly what you'd like to say. Then tell them what you really meant to say. Now THAT'S self-confidence. Be firm if a board member tries to rattle your cage. Firm doesn't mean inflexible—change your mind if you need to—just don't do it every other sentence. You want to avoid being labeled "wishy-washy."

Ready, Set, GO

You are as ready as you'll ever be if you follow these suggestions. There are no secrets to give away when it comes to oral interview boards. You can't change your past, your job history, or your educational status, your personality, or the job you did on your Personal History Statement. You can't fake maturity if you are not a mature individual. But you can put your best foot forward, fight for your cause, and be as well-prepared as possible.

If you follow the tips you've learned, you'll avoid making many of the mistakes that will eliminate other well-qualified candidates. You will also be ahead of the applicant who has the same qualifications you have, but who doesn't have a clue as to how to prepare for an oral interview board.

THE INSIDE TRACK

Who:	Jeffrey Knipp
What:	Deputy Sheriff
Where:	Audrain County Sheriff's Department in Mexico, Missouri
How long:	Over three years
Degree:	Graduate of the Law Enforcement Training Academy at the University of Missouri-Columbia, School of Law/Extension Division

Insider's Advice

My grandfather was a police officer years ago, before I was born. He always had a great deal of respect towards law enforcement in general. I guess I wanted to make him proud by following in his footsteps, but I also knew that it was a job in which I could do some good for my community.

Law enforcement is a challenging career. You'll meet some of the best people you will ever know, as well as the worst. There will be times of great joy and there will be times when you have mountains of paperwork. Don't let your personal beliefs interfere with your decisions; remember and abide by the law. A friend may not always be a friend when you are looking at the law from opposite sides. The most important advice that I can give is CYA (cover your a_ _).

Insider's Take on the Future

A typical day in this line of work includes serving both civil and criminal papers, arresting persons with and without warrants, responding to 911 emergency calls, responding to all criminal matters. There will be mountains of paper work, testifying in court, patrolling the 700 miles of roadway in my county, vacation home checks, business checks, surveillances, and marijuana eradication.

I love my job. I have a great sense of freedom and an ability to serve and protect the people in my county.

APPENDIX A

Your career search is not complete without a visit to the World Wide Web. Below is a list of law enforcement Web sites ranging from local, state, and federal sites to private Web pages maintained by law enforcement professionals. You'll also find a list of search engines, their addresses, and search tips to help you surf the Net.

USING THE NET TO CATCH YOUR DREAM

Whether you own one, borrow a buddy's, or dash to the public library to use their equipment, you should find a way to make friends with a PC (personal computer). A PC is a fantastic tool you can use to supplement your search for the right law enforcement job because it gives you access to the Internet.

Just in case you aren't familiar with some of the terminology, the Internet was created not too long ago as a defense project, and has since become the world's largest computer network. Through the Internet you can access the World Wide Web, a multimedia application that combines video, graphics, text, and sound. On the Web you'll find over 50,000 specific "sites" sponsored by various organizations and individuals.

New law enforcement Web sites are popping up on the Web every day as more and more departments catch on to the popularity of the "Net," as the Internet is affectionately known. And they're liking it! Police and sheriff's departments, state troopers, and government agencies like the FBI, are discovering the advantages of posting information on their Web sites for all to see...and download. Some agencies not only provide general information about their departments, but they also have their entire application process available for your inspection. You can even request applications from various sites while you are surfing the Web. Some federal sites allow you to apply for positions while you are on-line!

Andrea Richeson, a librarian for the State of Texas Technology Information Center, has advice for law enforcement job hunters:

> Ask a librarian for help! Even if your community does not have on-line access, you can probably get help and maybe even on-line access from county, state, federal, college, and university libraries. Look in your phone book's blue pages for contact information. Librarians can help you learn how to use the computer and/or print resources to help you find the information you need. If you are doing the searching yourself, the easiest way to gather information about law enforcement sites is to use search engines. Once you start pulling up Web sites with search engines, you'll see that they are linked to other law enforcement sites, and you'll be able to go on from there.

More information on search engines is available at the end of this chapter.

There are drawbacks to the Internet, though. Like most highways, the information highway is subject to traffic jams and sometimes it's difficult to get "on." As more and more users log on to their Internet providers, the speed at which you can use the Web often gets slower and slower. So, although this is a wonderful way to conduct your career search, you have to allow yourself plenty of time in front of the screen.

Listed below are a few sites worth checking out. Reaching these sites is just like finding someone's house—you need to know the address to get there. Once you are on the Net, you'll need a site's URL (Universal Resource Locator) address to find your way there. If you are totally in the dark about the Internet, don't forget to ask your local librarian for help. The library probably has a computer or two hooked up to the Internet for the public's use. And they'll certainly have plenty of books on the subject! Community colleges, community education classes, and universities are also great places to find access to the Internet.

We've provided a few addresses to give your search a jump start. Once you get to the URL address listed below, you'll see links to take you to an endless array of relevant sites.

Cop Net & Police Resource List

URL Address: *http://police.sas.ab.ca*

This is the premiere site for police-specific data. The most notable feature of Cop Net is that it gives you access to individual police departments. No two sites are identical, but most offer key background information and contact names. Included are links to city/county/state police departments, campus police departments, U.S. federal government agencies, military agencies, international agencies, commercial sites, and diverse public information and law enforcement association sites. (Note: Cop Net also features a private "Officers-Only Area" which you can tap into after *you* are a cop and get the password.)

Law Enforcement Sites on the Web

URL Address: *http://www.geopages.com/CapitolHill/1814/ira.html*

This site was developed by a licensed peace officer who has taught at the Lamar University Institute of Technology and the Criminal Justice Training Center's Regional Police Academy in Beaumont, Texas. It is billed as "possibly the largest collection of law enforcement sites on the Web." That's the plus side—all the other sites can be accessed from here. However, because it is such a large site, it can be time-consuming to use. A search function helps, allowing you to narrow your search by using key words (such as "police") that describe your particular interests.

Federal Government Sites

URL Address: *http://www.lib.lsu.edu/gov/fedgov.html*

Every branch of the federal government and federal agency can be found at this URL address: the Departments of Justice, Defense, Labor, etc., as well as federal courts, independent agencies and other government indexes. You'll see links to the DEA, the U.S. Marshals Service, and the FBI. You can even get to Congress and the White House for information about current legislative activity, transcripts of speeches, and other data. Just keep scrolling down the list and click on the topic you need.

International Sites

URL Address: *http://www.acsp.uic.edu/index.html*

You can explore the field of criminal justice worldwide from this site, which is organized by the following categories: publications, training, conferences, consulting services, and other criminal justice sites. The three "e-zine" publications featured here make for good reading with their on-line articles about policing and other law enforcement topics. "CJ The Americas On-Line" covers the U.S. and other North and South American countries. Also available are "CJ International" and "CJ Europe."

Internet Search Engines

Alta Vista: *http://www.altavista.digital.com*

Ask Jeeves: *http://www.askjeeves.com/*

GovBot: *http://cobar.cs.umass.edu/ciirdemo/Govbot/*
    (Developed by the Center for Intelligent Information Retrieval. You'll find over 535,000 Web pages from U.S. government and military sites.)

HotBot: *http://www.hotbot.com*

Inference Find: *http://www.inference.com/ifind/*

InfoSeek: *http://www.infoseek.com*

Lycos: *http://www.lycos.com*

Northern Light: *http://www.nlsearch.com/*

Yahoo!: *http://www.yahoo.com*

Search Tips

The Internet isn't perfect, as you can imagine. Problems do occur, such as links that don't work and servers that are too busy to let you continue your search. If you find you cannot get into a Web site, or a link that you've found on a Web site doesn't work, then you might consider choosing another Web site and trying their link to the location you want. For example, you are browsing through Cop Net and you see a link to the FBI's home page. You click on the site, but it tells you this site is unavailable. Choose another URL address listed in this section (or one you have found on your own) and use the link to the FBI's home page you find there. Or, you can go to a search engine like *Yahoo* and put in the key words "FBI" to see if *Yahoo* can find the FBI's home page for you. Your key word search should turn up all sorts of links!

In addition to Web sites, the Internet connects you to electronic mail (e-mail), USENET bulletin boards, and electronic discussion groups. Through these services you can have on-line "conversations" with people in the law enforcement field. Or you can simply read the many articles, press releases, and other electronic notices that are posted—including job openings. Both the Internet and the Web can be sources of valuable information for your career.

APPENDIX B

This appendix contains a list of addresses and telephone numbers for FBI field offices in major U.S. cities and in Puerto Rico.

FBI FIELD OFFICES

The FBI has 56 field offices in the U.S. and in Puerto Rico. Check with the location nearest you for recruiting information. The offices are listed alphabetically by city.

Federal Bureau of Investigation
Suite 502, James T. Foley Bldg.
445 Broadway
Albany, New York 12207
(518) 465-7551

Federal Bureau of Investigation
Suite 300
415 Silver Avenue, Southwest
Albuquerque, New Mexico 87102
(505) 224-2000

Federal Bureau of Investigation
101 East Sixth Avenue
Anchorage, Alaska 99501
(907) 258-5322

Federal Bureau of Investigation
Suite 400
2635 Century Parkway, Northeast
Atlanta, Georgia 30345
(404) 679-9000

Federal Bureau of Investigation
7142 Ambassador Road
Baltimore, Maryland 21244-2754
(410) 265-8080

Federal Bureau of Investigation
Room 1400
2121 8th Avenue N
Birmingham, Alabama 35203
(205) 252-7705

Federal Bureau of Investigation
Suite 600
One Center Plaza
Boston, Massachusetts 02108
(617) 742-5533

Federal Bureau of Investigation
One FBI Plaza
Buffalo, New York 14202-2698
(716) 856-7800

Federal Bureau of Investigation
Suite 900
400 South Tyron Street
Charlotte, North Carolina 28285
(704) 377-9200

Federal Bureau of Investigation
Room 905
E.M. Dirksen Federal Office Building
219 South Dearborn Street
Chicago, Illinois 60604
(312) 431-1333

Federal Bureau of Investigation
Room 9023
550 Main Street
Cincinnati, Ohio 45273-8501
(513)421-4310

Federal Bureau of Investigation
Room 3005
Federal Office Building
1240 East 9th Street
Cleveland, Ohio 44199-9912
(216) 522-1400

Federal Bureau of Investigation
Room 1357
1835 Assembly Street
Columbia, South Carolina 29201
(803) 254-3011

Federal Bureau of Investigation
Room 300
1801 North Lamar
Dallas, Texas 75202
(214) 720-2200

Federal Bureau of Investigation
Federal Office Building, Suite 1823
1961 Stout Street, 18th Floor
Denver, Colorado 80294
(303) 629-7171

Federal Bureau of Investigation
26th. Floor, P. V. McNamara FOB
477 Michigan Avenue
Detroit, Michigan 48226
(313) 965-2323

Federal Bureau of Investigation
Suite C-600
700 East San Antonio Avenue
El Paso, Texas 79901-7020
(915) 533-7451

Federal Bureau of Investigation
Room 4307, Kalanianaole FOB
300 Ala Moana Boulevard
Honolulu, Hawaii 96850
(808) 521-1411

Federal Bureau of Investigation
Room 200
2500 East TC Jester
Houston, Texas 77008-1300
(713) 868-2266

Federal Bureau of Investigation
Room 679, FOB
575 North Pennsylvania Street
Indianapolis, Indiana 46204
(317) 639-3301

Federal Bureau of Investigation
Room 1553, FOB
100 West Capitol Street
Jackson, Mississippi 39269
(601) 948-5000

Federal Bureau of Investigation
Suite 200
7820 Arlington Expressway
Jacksonville, Florida 32211
(904) 721-1211

Federal Bureau of Investigation
Room 300, U.S. Courthouse
811 Grand Avenue
Kansas City, Missouri 64106
(816) 221-6100

Federal Bureau of Investigation
Suite 600, John J. Duncan FOB
710 Locust Street
Knoxville, Tennessee 37902
(423) 544-0751

Federal Bureau of Investigation
700 East Charleston Boulevard
Las Vegas, Nevada 89101
(702) 385-1281

Federal Bureau of Investigation
Suite 200
Two Financial Centre
10825 Financial Centre Parkway
Little Rock, Arkansas 72211-3552
(501) 221-9100

Federal Bureau of Investigation
Suite 1700, FOB
11000 Wilshire Boulevard
Los Angeles, California 90024
(310) 477-6565

Federal Bureau of Investigation
Room 500
600 Martin Luther King Jr. Place
Louisville, Kentucky 40202
(502) 583-3941

Federal Bureau of Investigation
Suite 3000, Eagle Crest Bldg.
225 North Humphreys Blvd.
Memphis, Tennessee 38120-2107
(901) 747-4300

Federal Bureau of Investigation
16320 Northwest Second Avenue
North Miami Beach, Florida 33169
(305) 944-9101

Federal Bureau of Investigation
Suite 600
330 East Kilbourn Avenue
Milwaukee, Wisconsin 53202-6627
(414) 276-4684

Federal Bureau of Investigation
Suite 1100
111 Washington Avenue, South
Minneapolis, Minnesota 55401
(612) 376-3200

Federal Bureau of Investigation
One St. Louis Centre
1 St. Louis Street, 3rd Floor
Mobile, Alabama 36602
(334) 438-3674

Federal Bureau of Investigation
1 Gateway Center, 22nd Floor
Newark, New Jersey 07102-9889
(201) 622-5613

Federal Bureau of Investigation
Room 535, FOB
150 Court Street
New Haven, Connecticut 06510
(203) 777-6311

Federal Bureau of Investigation
Suite 2200
1250 Poydras Street
New Orleans, Louisiana 70113-1829
(504) 522-4671

Federal Bureau of Investigation
26 Federal Plaza, 23rd Floor
New York, New York 10278
212-384-1000

Federal Bureau of Investigation
150 Corporate Boulevard
Norfolk, Virginia 23502
(804) 455-0100

Federal Bureau of Investigation
Suite 1600
50 Penn Place
Oklahoma City, Oklahoma 73118
(405) 290-7770

Federal Bureau of Investigation
10755 Burt Street
Omaha, Nebraska 68114
(402) 493-8688

Federal Bureau of Investigation
8th Floor
William J. Green Jr. FOB
600 Arch Street
Philadelphia, Pennsylvania 19106
(215) 829-2700

Federal Bureau of Investigation
Suite 400
201 East Indianola Avenue
Phoenix, Arizona 85012
(602) 279-5511

Federal Bureau of Investigation
Suite 300
U.S. Post Office Building
700 Grant Street
Pittsburgh, Pennsylvania 15219
(412) 471-2000

Federal Bureau of Investigation
Suite 401, Crown Plaza Building
1500 Southwest 1st Avenue
Portland, Oregon 97201
(503) 224-4181

Federal Bureau of Investigation
111 Greencourt Road
Richmond, Virginia 23228
(804) 261-1044

Federal Bureau of Investigation
4500 Orange Grove Avenue
Sacramento, California 95841-4205
(916) 481-9110

Federal Bureau of Investigation
Room 2704
L. Douglas Abram Federal Bldg.
1520 Market Street
St. Louis, Missouri 63103
(314) 241-5357

Federal Bureau of Investigation
Suite 1200, 257 Towers Bldg.
257 East, 200 South
Salt Lake City, Utah 84111
(801) 579-1400

Federal Bureau of Investigation
Suite 200
U.S. Post Office & Courthouse Bldg.
615 East Houston Street
San Antonio, Texas 78205
(210) 225-6741

Federal Bureau of Investigation
Federal Office Building
9797 Aero Drive
San Diego, California 92123-1800
(619) 565-1255

Federal Bureau of Investigation
450 Golden Gate Avenue, 13th Floor
San Francisco, California 94102-9523
(415) 553-7400

Federal Bureau of Investigation
Room 526, U.S. Federal Bldg.
150 Carlos Chardon Avenue
Hato Rey
San Juan, Puerto Rico 00918-1716
(809) 754-6000

Federal Bureau of Investigation
Room 710
915 Second Avenue
Seattle, Washington 98174-1096
(206) 622-0460

Federal Bureau of Investigation
Suite 400
400 West Monroe Street
Springfield, Illinois 62704
(217) 522-9675

Federal Bureau of Investigation
Room 610, FOB
500 Zack Street
Tampa, Florida 33602
(813) 273-4566

Federal Bureau of Investigation
Washington Metropolitan Field Office
1900 Half Street, SW
Washington, D.C. 20024
(202) 252-7801

APPENDIX C

This appendix contains a list of useful books that will give you more specific advice on areas with which you need help.

ADDITIONAL RESOURCES

For additional information on the topics discussed in this book, refer to the following reading lists, which are organized by subject.

Colleges

The College Board, *The College Handbook 1998*. 35th Ed. New York: College Entrance Exam Board. 1997.

Peterson's Guide to Two-Year Colleges 1998: The Only Guide to More than 1,500 Community and Junior Colleges. Princeton, NJ: Peterson's. 1997.

The Princeton Review, *The Complete Book of Colleges 1998*. New York: Random House, The Princeton Review. 1997.

Financial Aid

Chany, Kalman A. and Geoff Martz, *Student Advantage Guide to Paying for College 1997 Edition*. New York: Random House, The Princeton Review. 1997.

College School Service, *College Costs & Financial Aid Handbook*. 18th Ed. New York: The College Entrance Examination Board. 1998.

Davis, Kristen, *Financing College: How to Use Savings, Financial Aid, Scholarships, and Loans to Afford the School of Your Choice*. Washington, DC: Random House. 1996.

See also Scholarships section, below.

Job Hunting

Bernstein, Sara T., and Kathleen M. Savage, Eds. *Vocational Careers Sourcebook*. New York: Gale Research, International Thomson Publishers. 1996.

Bureau of Labor Statistics, *Dictionary of Occupational Titles*. 4th Ed. Vol. 1, 2. Bureau of Labor Statistics. 1991.

Bureau of Labor Statistics, *Occupational Outlook Handbook 1996–1997*. Internet address: http://www.bls.gov

Cubbage, Sue A. and Marcia P. Williams, *The 1996 National Job Hotline Directory*. New York: McGraw-Hill. 1996.

Sonneblick, Carol, Kim Crabbe, and Michaele Basciano, *Job Hunting Made Easy*. New York: LearningExpress. 1997.

Law Enforcement Exams

Corrections Officer: California. New York: LearningExpress, 1996.

Corrections Officer: Florida. New York: LearningExpress, 1996.

Corrections Officer: New Jersey. New York: LearningExpress, 1996.

Corrections Officer: New York. New York: LearningExpress, 1996.

Corrections Officer: Texas. New York: LearningExpress, 1996.
Police Officer Exam: California. New York: LearningExpress, 1996.

Police Officer Exam: Chicago. New York: LearningExpress, 1997.

Police Officer Exam: Florida. New York: LearningExpress, 1996.

Police Officer Exam: Massachusetts. New York: LearningExpress, 1997.

Police Officer Exam: New Jersey. New York: LearningExpress, 1997.

Police Officer Exam: New York City. New York: LearningExpress, 1998.

Police Officer Exam: Suffolk County. New York: LearningExpress, 1996.

Police Officer Exam: Texas. New York: LearningExpress, 1996.

Police Officer Exam: The Midwest. New York: LearningExpress, 1997.

Police Officer Exam: The South. New York: LearningExpress, 1997.

State Police Exam: California. New York: LearningExpress, 1996.

State Police Exam: Massachusetts. New York: LearningExpress, 1997.

State Police Exam: New Jersey. New York: LearningExpress, 1997.

State Police Exam: New York. New York: LearningExpress, 1996.

State Police Exam: Texas. New York: LearningExpress, 1996.

> To order any LearningExpress publication, call toll-free:
> **1–888–551–5627**

Scholarship Guides

Cassidy, Daniel J., *The Scholarship Book: The Complete Guide to Private-Sector Scholarships, Grants, and Loans for Undergraduates.* Englewood Cliffs, NJ: Prentice Hall. 1996.

Ragins, Marianne, *Winning Scholarships for College: An Insider's Guide.* New York: Henry Holt & Co. 1994.

Scholarships, Grants & Prizes: Guide to College Financial Aid From Private Sources. Princeton, NJ: Peterson's. 1998.

Schwartz, John, *College Scholarships and Financial Aid.* New York: Simon & Schuster, Macmillan. 1995.

Scholarships 1998. New York: Simon & Schuster, Kaplan. 1997.

Studying

Chesla, Elizabeth, *Read Better, Remember More.* New York: LearningExpress. 1997.

Chesla, Elizabeth, *Reading Comprehension Success in 20 Minutes a Day.* 2nd ed. New York: LearningExpress. 1998.

Coman, Marcia J. and Kathy L Heavers, *How to Improve Your Study Skills.* 2nd ed. Lincolnwood, IL: NTC Publishing. 1998.

Fry, Ron, *Ron Fry's How to Study Program.* 4th ed. New Jersey: Career Press. 1996.

Meyers, Judith N., *Vocabulary and Spelling Success in 20 Minutes a Day.* 2nd ed. New York: LearningExpress, 1998.

Robinovitz, Judith, *Practical Math Success in 20 Minutes a Day.* 2nd ed. New York: LearningExpress. 1998.

Silver, Theodore M.D., J.D. *The Princeton Review Study Smart: Hands-On Nuts-and-Bolts Techniques for Earning Higher Grades.* New York: Villard Books. 1995.

Gail Wood, *How to Study.* New York: LearningExpress. 1997.

Test Help

ACT: Powerful Strategies to Help You Score Higher. 1998 Edition. Kaplan. New York: Simon & Schuster. 1997.

ASVAB: Armed Services Vocational Aptitude Battery. New York: LearningExpress. 1997.

Katyman, John and Adam Robinson, *Cracking the SAT & PSAT 1998 Edition.* New York: Random House, The Princeton Review. 1997.

Meyers, Judith N., *The Secrets of Taking Any Test.* New York: LearningExpress. 1997.

Previous edition SAT and ACT test preparation books should also be available at your local library.

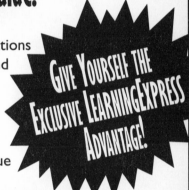

Order Form

CALIFORNIA EXAMS

___ @ $35.00   CA Police Officer
___ @ $35.00   CA State Police
___ @ $35.00   CA Corrections Officer
___ @ $20.00   CA Law Enforcement Career Guide
___ @ $35.00   CA Firefighter
___ @ $30.00   CA Postal Worker
___ @ $35.00   CA Allied Health

NEW JERSEY EXAMS

___ @ $35.00   NJ Police Officer
___ @ $35.00   NJ State Police
___ @ $35.00   NJ Corrections Officer
___ @ $20.00   NJ Law Enforcement Career Guide
___ @ $35.00   NJ Firefighter
___ @ $30.00   NJ Postal Worker
___ @ $35.00   NJ Allied Health

TEXAS EXAMS

___ @ $35.00   TX Police Officer
___ @ $30.00   TX State Police
___ @ $35.00   TX Corrections Officer
___ @ $20.00   TX Law Enforcement Career Guide
___ @ $35.00   TX Firefighter
___ @ $30.00   TX Postal Worker
___ @ $32.50   TX Allied Health

NEW YORK EXAMS

___ @ $30.00   NYC/Nassau County Police Officer
___ @ $30.00   Suffolk County Police Officer
___ @ $30.00   New York City Firefighter
___ @ $35.00   NY State Police
___ @ $35.00   NY Corrections Officer
___ @ $20.00   NY Law Enforcement Career Guide
___ @ $35.00   NY Firefighter
___ @ $30.00   NY Postal Worker
___ @ $35.00   NY Allied Health
___ @ $30.00   NY Postal Worker

MASSACHUSETTS EXAMS

___ @ $30.00   MA Police Officer
___ @ $30.00   MA State Police Exam
___ @ $30.00   MA Allied Health

FLORIDA EXAMS

___ @ $35.00   FL Police Officer
___ @ $35.00   FL Corrections Officer
___ @ $20.00   FL Law Enforcement Career Guide
___ @ $30.00   FL Postal Worker
___ @ $32.50   FL Allied Health

ILLINOIS EXAMS

___ @ $25.00   Chicago Police Officer
___ @ $25.00   Illinois Allied Health

The MIDWEST EXAMS

(Illinois, Indiana, Michigan, Minnesota, Ohio, and Wisconsin)

___ @ $30.00   Midwest Police Officer Exam
___ @ $30.00   Midwest Firefighter Exam

The SOUTH EXAMS

(Alabama, Arkansas, Georgia, Louisiana, Mississippi, North Carolina, South Carolina, and Virginia)

___ @ $25.00   The South Police Officer Exam
___ @ $25.00   The South Firefighter Exam

NATIONAL EDITIONS

___ @ $14.95   ASVAB (Armed Services Vocational Aptitude Battery)
___ @ $12.95   U.S. Postal Worker Exam
___ @ $15.00   Federal Clerical Worker Exam
___ @ $12.95   Bus Operator Exam
___ @ $12.95   Sanitation Worker Exam
___ @ $20.00   Allied Health Entrance Exams

NATIONAL CERTIFICATION EXAMS

___ @ $20.00   Home Health Aide Certification Exam
___ @ $20.00   Nursing Assistant Certification Exam
___ @ $20.00   EMT-Basic Certification Exam

CAREER STARTERS

___ @ $14.95   Computer Technician
___ @ $14.95   Health Care
___ @ $14.95   Paralegal
___ @ $14.95   Administrative Assistant/Secretary
___ @ $14.00   Civil Service

To Order, Call TOLL-FREE: 1-888-551-JOBS, Dept. A040

Or, mail this order form with your check or money order* to:
LearningExpress, Dept. A040, 20 Academy Street, Norwalk, CT 06850

Please allow at least 2-4 weeks for delivery. Prices subject to change without notice   *NY, CT, & MD residents add appropriate sales tax

LEARNINGEXPRESS
An Affiliate Company of Random House, Inc.